I AM
Your
MUSTARD SEED…

I AM

Your

MUSTARD SEED…

A Faith Walk Through a Barren Land

LIZA PAIGE

XULON PRESS

Xulon Press
2301 Lucien Way #415
Maitland, FL 32751
407.339.4217
www.xulonpress.com

Unless otherwise indicated, Scripture quotations taken from the King James Version (KJV) – *public domain*.

Edited by Xulon Press

Printed in the United States of America.

ISBN-13: 978-1-5456-8058-2

CONTENTS

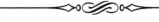

In Loving Memory of:
Delores Ann
May 24, 1940

August 21, 2001

To Alexandria

You are the third in a generation of mother, daughter, and granddaughter. As I had with my mother and my grandmother, you have a great legacy in your grandmother and me; honor it, cherish it, be true to it.

Although you were only twelve when your Nauni went home to be with the Lord, you spent all of your young life with her. You were blessed with the opportunity to bring her much joy and happiness, as she did you, by spending time with you and imparting much wisdom in you at such a young age.

Thank you for being such a blessing to her, and most of all thank you for being such a blessing to me. Now that you are a woman and mother coming into your own, I appreciate you for your godly wisdom, encouragement, support, and prayers. For many years, I've heard you say, "Mommy, you are my hero," but I now say to you, thank you for being mine!

I love you with all of my heart!

To Shellie Marie

I was given the blessed privilege of naming you when you first came out of Mommy's womb. What an extraordinary privilege it has been to be your older and only sibling, to set some of the positive examples for your path early in your life.

Thank you for allowing me to come to you when I had no other human comfort during one of the most difficult times of my life. Thank you for trusting me with the care of Mommy during one of the most difficult times of your life. I know the difficulty for you was not being able to always be there physically.

You are my sister and the most important thing that you did and could have ever done for me during those times was to be. God created us as sisters and it is a bond that is everlasting.

I loved you in the beginning, I love you now and will love you always!

ACKNOWLEDGMENTS

To my Heavenly Father, my Daddy, my Friend, and without the guidance of the Holy Spirit, this project would never have been possible. It is because of my Lord and my Savior that this book has been written. It is for Him that I write these words, that He would get the glory out of this book. It is because of Him that I can relive this experience through these pages from my brokenness, that only He could heal. Through my pain, that only He could medicate and finally through my mind, that only He could renew that I could relive these memories and see joy.

To the men and women of God the Father has allowed to impart the knowledge, wisdom, and the things of Him into my life, I truly bless God for each and every one of you.

For verily I say unto you, "If ye have faith as a grain of mustard seed, ye shall say unto this mountain, Remove hence to yonder place; and it shall remove; and nothing shall be impossible unto you."
Matthew 17:20

INTRODUCTION

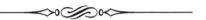

While writing this book, there was clearly some revelation that came forth for me during the process. The following statements are in no way meant to minimize the experience of a person afflicted with a terminal illness. However, they are meant to recognize the person or persons who have seen and cared for the afflicted one as I did for my mother, through their pain, their suffering, their heartache, their uncertainty, and, through the effects of radiation, chemotherapy, medication, hair loss, and weight loss. In my case, even when the afflicted one succumbs to death.

I have come to realize I am a survivor. Although I am one of a different kind, I am a survivor. I experienced everything that this enemy cancer brought with it, with the exception of its physical aspects. The disease itself did not attack my body, but it attacked my ability to function like it attacked my mother's ability to function. It attacked my ability to work, as it attacked my mother's ability to work. It attacked my ability to eat and sleep, just as it attacked those same abilities in her. It attacked my ability to help the person that I loved so deeply and made me watch her pain and suffering, while dying daily in a battle for her life. She died, I lived, and I am surviving the emotions of pain and suffering, knowing that I did all that I could, and then finally surviving the loss.

This book is for those of you who may be going through or have come through a storm of life, having a loved one that you've been given the privilege of caring for until their healing or in some cases, until their last breath. I bless my Heavenly Father and honor Him for giving me the supernatural strength that I needed and then allowing me to put it to use in caring for my mother, one of His children, until she took her last breath and went home.

To the readers of these pages, be blessed in knowing God truly is with you and will never leave you or forsake you, especially when He gives you the capacity to weather a storm of this magnitude that you can't see your way through.

Chapter 1

I Already Knew

I called from work once again and heard the cough over the phone as she answered.

"How are you feeling?" I asked with building concern in my voice. "Mommy, it has been three weeks that you've had this cold and you need to call the doctor and get something for it."

"I know, I know," she answered.

Finally, when I got home that afternoon I had put my things down in the den of our two-family house and went up to the second floor to mom's. I could hear her coughing as I came through the back door and called for my daughter Alexandria, who was ten. Alex would get off the school bus at the corner and would go up to her Naunie's house until I arrived home from work. "Naunie" is what she called my mother instead of "Nana" or "Grandma." My mom liked that name because it gave her more than an identity; it gave her character, a uniqueness with her granddaughter.

I went into the den where Alex and my stepfather watched television. I gave Alex a hug and kiss.

"How was your day, sweetie?"

"It was fine, Mommy."

We then began the ritual of me asking if she had homework and her telling me what it was and us getting it started. Probably the same ritual or close to what every parent of a school-aged child goes through at the beginning of the evening. I then proceeded into my mother's bedroom where she was watching television in bed.

"I called the doctor today."

"I'm glad, Mom," I replied with relief. "What did she say?"

"She called in a prescription. Can you go and pick it up?"

"Sure, let me just get settled and I will throw on some jeans and run over there."

The pharmacy was about fifteen minutes away from our house. I was a bit fatigued from the events of my workday. It was 1999 and I was working on a Y2K project, which was intense due to the nature of the project and how dependent our company was on technology. I picked up the prescription which was a mixture of Tylenol and Codeine from the doctor which I knew would help with the cough and begin the healing process so that I could see my mother out of bed and up and running around like she normally was in her little green Subaru. Mom had been retired for the last eight years and had gone through trying times since her retirement. She often likened herself to Job of the Bible, not that there was a real comparison in terms of all that Job lost between loved ones and possessions. Yet, I could understand how she would feel some similarities. In the eight years that she had been retired, she had been ill on a number of occasions when one would have expected her to be living the good life, not having to get up to report to work, but using her time the way she wanted to, for purposes of ministry. Mom had given her life to the Lord as a promise to Him for saving her life.

Earlier, in 1991, when my daughter was two years old, my mom was great about being a help to me since I had become a single parent from the time that Alex was one year old. She would pick Alex up for me from daycare if I was held later than usual at work. The daycare that she attended had a summer program for kids as well, which made it convenient for me as a full-time working mom. However, there was a two-week break during summer sessions at which time parents of the program had to make other arrangements for their children. Fortunately, I was able to take a week off from my job, but there was no way that I was able to secure two consecutive weeks off at one time. My mom, being the wonderful and true Naunie that she was, stepped in and took Alex for me for the first week. I remember her not feeling well during that whole week. In fact, I was glad when the first week was over, because I felt a bit guilty and wanted to give her a chance to rest. She had been suffering from stomach pain throughout the week, but had no other real symptoms. The pain itself was enough to me, but she felt that she needed more to go by before going to the doctor. I remember us getting into a bit of an argument because I knew she was sick but could not force her to go to the doctor.

Mom's stoic nature would keep her from attending to herself in many cases in a timely fashion. Finally, as we were into the second week of Alex's two-week daycare break, she called me on the telephone downstairs, "I think I need to go the doctor now."

I rushed upstairs since Alex was still sleeping and asked her what had happened. She replied in a weak voice, "I just went to the bathroom and my stool is black."

I had no idea what this meant, but it sounded serious enough to me, so I rushed downstairs, woke Alex up, got her dressed, and called the doctor's office to alert them of our arrival. I was able to leave Alex with my stepfather while I went to the doctor with Mom. We arrived at the doctor's office about fifteen minutes later, and they took her in right away. I remember that her regular doctor had been out, but Sarah, a new nurse practitioner, had taken over the doctor's patients, which was customary to this particular HMO. If need be, the doctor on duty would see my mother as well.

I was unable to go into the examining room, so I waited in the patient waiting area to hear something from the medical staff. The wait felt as though it was forever, but I looked up and Sarah was before me with a look on her face that told me to prepare for the worst.

"Your mother is very sick; we need to transport her over to the hospital emergency room immediately. We have already called ahead and they are expecting her. She will be transported by ambulance."

I went numb as I tried to focus on what she said. She suggested I drive my car over instead of taking the ambulance with my mom because she knew they would keep her.

"Your mother is bleeding internally and has lost several pints of blood and her hematocrit level is approximately twenty-six, while, if normal, it would be closer to forty-five."

As I traveled over to the hospital by car, all I could think was, *is this it? Is this the end of my mother?* I did not believe that this would be the case, but I was so stunned from the rush of information that I was not sure what to think.

When I arrived at the hospital, I called my sister and my stepfather and they alerted family members of my mother's condition. The emergency room doctor walked up to me, introduced himself, and said, "A blood transfusion has to be done immediately."

"Can my family members donate blood?"

"There is no time to receive blood from family members because of the extensive testing that would need to be done in order to donate any blood. Your mother has only hours to live if not given the transfusion immediately. We have not located where the origin of the bleeding is."

Mom spent one week in the Intensive Care Unit and three to four more in a room on one of the floors. She was diagnosed with a Duodenal Ulcer, which caused the internal bleeding.

Upon her release from the hospital, she was miraculously given a clean bill of health. She was told to be careful in taking any medication that could cause bleeding to the stomach. But the most miraculous part of her experience was that she said, "I told God that if I ever made it out of this hospital, that I would dedicate my life to Him." And so, she lived up to her end of the bargain. She went to church the following Sunday, and when the altar call was made, her original plan was to go up for prayer, but God had another plan. She found herself mumbling the words "I want to be saved" when she got to the altar, and she gave her life to Christ.

From that point on, my mom lived for the Lord with excitement in her heart, and excitement in her step. She was full of joy and wanted everyone to know why. She had been healed and set free and she was not hiding it. I had not seen my mother so happy, lighthearted, and full of determination to live in a long time. It was amazing to watch and even more amazing to hear her give her testimony of life and her promise to God to other people. I had lived through it with her, but to hear her tell it still gave me goosebumps. It made people understand why she could serve a God that no one had ever seen and made many of them want to know Him like she did.

Mom immediately went to work for the Lord at our church. At that time, we attended a small church that my great-uncle had founded and pastored until his death. He had passed it down to a young man that had served as a youth minister when we were children. Pastor Reason, whom my mother referred to as "Danny", was truly respected and loved by her. He was the young man who would come in rain, snow, sleet, and hail to pick up her children for Sunday school in the church van even though she didn't attend church at that time. He would pick us up for youth activities sponsored by the church, and run himself tirelessly, all to be a blessing to the families that he served. As a new Christian, this church was the right place for us to attend as a family.

As much as she was brought to Christ through this experience, I too recommitted my life to the Lord. I had grown up in the church as a child and in my early teens, but left in my late teens and spent most of my early adult years out of church. In looking back at those years, I realize God had been wooing me back to Him through many experiences. I saw it and knew He had tried to beckon me back to Him, but I ignored all of the prior invitations. At that time, I believed if I ever went back to a church, I would never leave. The problem was I also believed that in order not to disappoint God,

I had to get my life right first. Before I went back, I had to clean up: stop drinking, stop smoking, stop doing everything that God would not approve of so that I would not disappoint Him. That was the lie that Satan wanted me to believe and the lie that can keep many of us from the freedom in giving our lives to the Lord.

Finally, the Lord had me. In fact, He had almost everyone in my immediate family. My sister had grown up in the church like me, but she never left. She hung in there, strong, praying that her family would come back, especially mom, and God answered her prayers.

Mom was so active in church. She was there when the doors of the church opened and when they closed. She was there for Sunday school, morning services, and weekly Bible study. She had joined the choir and had become one of the most joyous singers in the choir. She was so grateful for her new lease on life. She was not afraid to show it as she sang and cried and was filled with the love of the Lord. I can still think back on some of the songs she used to sing. People loved to watch her sing because she showed everyone how they too could be happy in Jesus.

She then got excited about other ways that she could serve the Lord and wanted to get on the missionary department of our church. She became a local missionary and poured all of the love that the Lord had given her into the work that she did and the people that she served. My mom had lost my grandmother, who died at the age of sixty-one, so she desperately missed having a mother figure in her life. She became a spiritual and surrogate daughter to the church mother at our church. Our church mother had never been blessed to have children from her womb, but truly was as much a mother to those that were sent into her life. Mother Sparks was wonderful. She and my mom would spend lots of time on the telephone. My mom would spend time at her home and they would go out and do many things together. "Momma," as my mother called her, was so close that when Mom could not get there to do things, I made my way to her. Not necessarily because I was asked, but it just felt like the connection was so great, it flowed onto me naturally. She had become like a grandmother to me. Even though I still had my grandparents on my father's side that I also visited and took my daughter to see, Mother Sparks was now a part of our family. Mother Sparks was also the head of the missionary department and a missionary extraordinaire. She too had a love of the Lord that illuminated wherever she went. She had a wonderful wisdom about her and had been through a lot in her life. She was in her late eighties and could tell a story or two. My mom adored this woman of God she had been blessed with in the absence of her natural mother.

As time went on, Mom read her Bible, prayed, and learned to live her life richer than ever before. Even when there was less in her pocket, there was so much more in her spirit that spilled into gladness, no matter the situation. She was at a point where she was active, mostly in church, but she also had a full-time career with the Department of Corrections. She had been with the Department of Corrections for almost twenty-three years. She had begun her career as a Correctional Officer when I was a teenager. I still have the pictures of her graduation. I used to get a chuckle out of my daughter, who, as a teenager, looking at my clothes in those pictures and realizing she had some of the same styles in her closet. I always told her that there was nothing new under the sun, history does indeed repeat itself.

Once mom retired from her twenty-three-year career with the Department of Corrections, she wanted to do a lot. She spent time at the church in a volunteer capacity with a local food program and made many visits to hospitals and homes. She had a great time in her retirement. She had retired early, so she had lots of energy to accomplish her goals.

I had finally returned home with the prescription that I had picked up for Mom's terrible cough, and was not overly concerned, but wanted her to feel better. In the past, our relationship had, at times, been strained even though we loved each other deeply. Satan was always on the prowl to sabotage our relationship. He had been striking at our relationship since my early teens and at one point, had accomplished a breakdown in our communication with one another. I found myself often crying before the Lord to heal the broken areas of our relationship. Only God could fix the brokenness that we had experienced between a mother and daughter. However, seeing my mom in this state softened me because I loved her and admired her strength and wanted to see her better.

I remember sitting with her after getting her a spoon to start the medication. "How long did the doctor say this would take to begin having an effect on your cough, Mom?"

"The doctor said that is should start working within a day or so. If not, to call her to make an appointment to come in and see her."

I checked on her once more that evening before she fell asleep.

The next morning, I immediately picked up the phone to call my mom to see how she was feeling. We usually talked early in the morning and then several times throughout the day.

She answered the phone, "Hello?" still sounding groggy.

"You're asleep. I will check in with you later in the day."

I called her around lunchtime and she still had a hacking cough. "Are you beginning to feel any better, Mom?"

"I don't really know, but let's give the medication some more time to work," she responded.

A few more days passed and I had become concerned with no change in mom's cough. As I sat at her bedside, I suggested she make an appointment to go to the doctor because we were about to travel for the holiday. It was December 15, 1999 and we were scheduled to go to Alabama to see my sister and her family for Christmas. I suggested she get a chest x-ray to make sure that she did not have pneumonia. Then, I heard in my spirit, "Cancer." I still remember the chill that I got when that word rushed through my spirit, and it must have shown on my face, because I so clearly remember her asking me what had flashed across my mind. I said, "Nothing really," not trying to lie, but certainly not to alarm her. The feeling I had received felt like when a fighter is in the boxing ring, and a punch comes out of nowhere and he has to shake it off. I knew it was not only a thought, or a whim—this was a warning to prepare me for what I now already knew.

Mom called me at work the next day to inform me that she had called the doctor's office to make an appointment because the medication did not seem to be working.

"Will you go with me?" she asked, and without hesitation, I asked, "When and what time?"

"It is tomorrow at 9:30 a.m."

I had plenty of accrued vacation time, so I planned to take the day off to go with her. I remember as I got up to pray the morning of the appointment, I did not pray specifically about the feeling that was in my spirit that had nearly knocked the wind out of me days before, but more for the doctor to find out what the problem was and to put the right people in place to give us what we needed. Well, as always God answers prayers. We may not always be happy with the answer, but He is faithful to answer.

Chapter 2

THE CONFIRMATION

W e arrived at the doctor's office for an early morning appointment on December 17, 1999, two days before we were scheduled to leave for Alabama.

I remember how much my mom had liked this particular doctor. She had not been my mother's primary care physician for a long time, but for the time that my mother had spent with her, she had shared the gospel of Jesus Christ with this woman, and it had made a difference. She cared for and respected my mother and it was apparent upon meeting her.

As we sat in the waiting room, I wondered whether we would have to cancel our trip in order for my mother to undergo further testing. My hope was that the worst case was that she had a form of treatable pneumonia. I thought about how adamant my sister had been about us coming down this year. I knew that I could not stay as long as I had hoped because of work. Her beseeching request was, "You guys have to come this year. Whatever it takes, let's make a way. This year, for some reason, it's really important." Little did she know how prophetic her words were, or maybe she was already aware of their importance.

We had already gone down for the x-ray and we finally got the okay to go back to the room and were instructed to wait there while the doctor reviewed the x-ray film. Mom and I waited for about fifteen minutes in the room and chatted about completing our packing, especially since the weather in Alabama would be different than Massachusetts. We heard a knock at the door and the doctor entered the room. The look on her face was one of grave concern. Yet she appeared genuinely surprised to have to deliver this type of news, as though her discovery had come as a shock even to her.

She said calmly, "You have a spot on your lung that we see on the x-ray." She showed us on the x-ray where it was located.

Mom gasped in shock, and in a childlike voice said, "Liza."

I was numb. What I had heard in my spirit had just been confirmed: my mother had cancer. I remember that being such a sobering moment. My first thoughts were, *okay, what do we need to do next because this is not going to happen and we give into it.* I took charge at that moment. I knew my mother had always been a strong woman, but I remember the whimper of my name when the doctor said the "C" word, and I grabbed her hand and said, "Mommy, it's going to be okay. Don't worry. It's going to be okay." I said it for both of us. I needed to hear it as much as she did.

The doctor wanted to give us time to make some decisions about our holiday plans, but wanted my mother to have a CT-scan done as soon as possible. I took the referral information that she gave us and we left the office.

The drive home was quiet, I could see the look of pain on my mom's face, one mixed with panic and distress. I, on the other hand, could only think of the next steps and how to beat this thing. It was not going to defeat us. It had to be beaten!

Upon our arrival to the house, we decided to sit in the quiet of the kitchen, drink a cup of tea, and talk. We began with prayer before we said anything further about the news we had just received. After which, my mom called my stepfather into the room, sat him down, and delivered the news. He was silent. He got up and walked into the other room. He needed to deal with the bullet that had just been shot into him in his own way.

We decided we would continue with our plans to travel to Alabama for the holiday. My sister and brother-in-law needed to be told of my mother's diagnosis and this would be the only time to tell them face-to-face before beginning the process of treating this disease that had attacked my mother's body.

Chapter 3

THE JOURNEY: PHASE I

We left as scheduled on the morning of December 19, to travel to Alabama for the holiday. I had taken the time prior to leaving to schedule an appointment for mom to have the CT-scan as soon as we returned back to Boston. Her CT-scan was scheduled for less than a week after our return from the holiday, but with enough time for me to schedule a few more days off in order to be with her during these appointments.

This Christmas holiday was going to be a solemn one, but it was good for all of us to be together. As my sister had so emphatically requested, we were all in Alabama for Christmas. We had arrived by train on December 20 and my sister and brother-in-law met us at the train station. My mother did not like to fly, so we took the train from Boston to Birmingham, which lasted approximately twenty-four hours. As we took the forty-minute drive from the train station to their home, Mom was still nursing her cough and feeling quite fatigued from both the lengthy trip and her condition.

As soon as we arrived at the house, Mom asked, "Would anyone mind if I went into the bedroom and rested for a while before dinner?" as if anyone would object.

"Of course we don't mind, Mom!" we all replied. "Go and rest and we'll wake you for dinner." She and my stepfather retreated to their bedroom to rest.

At about 6:30 that evening, my mom and stepfather emerged from their end of the house to join us. As we sat at the dinner table that evening laughing and reminiscing, my thoughts transitioned into solemn mode. It did not seem as though my mom's illness was a reality. She was diagnosed with lung cancer only five days prior and we now had to announce this harsh reality to my sister and brother-in-law. My daughter, only ten at the time, did not need to hear this devastating news yet, and my nephew who was only three was clearly unable to comprehend this information. The silence was deafening around the table after we shared the news. Gradually the conversation began again; some questions were asked, but none could be adequately answered since we had only received the diagnosis and the next appointment had been set.

When we returned home, I realized my stepfather was in no way ready to handle this situation with the sense of urgency that it demanded, and my sister was clearly too far away. I immediately went into advocate mode. Prior to the appointment for the CT-scan, I began doing research about lung cancer on the internet. The information that I found was quite depressing and the survival rate percentages were so low, I remember sitting at the computer crying and thinking, *is this all they have? Is there no more hope than what we are being given by these statistics?* Then, I was comforted by the Holy Spirit, remembering that the Lord is our hope. Was I worried? Absolutely! Was I scared? Without a doubt! But I knew from where I could draw my strength; I knew I could only draw strength for this type of battle from the Lord. No one else could comfort me; no one else could assure me I would make it through this with my mother but God.

The appointment day had arrived. We made sure that we had followed all of the procedures given to us to prepare prior to the appointment. It was an early morning appointment so the waiting area was quiet. I had no idea how long this would take, or what would be involved since I had no prior experience with this type of an appointment. I remembered to bring a few books to read while waiting for Mom; however, I was not sure how much I would be able to concentrate on their content.

After a few moments, the nurse came out and called me in to say Mom was having some difficulty with the CT-scan because the machine had her enclosed and she felt claustrophobic. I have never had a CT-scan, but even those that I spoke with after our experience that don't suffer from claustrophobia stated that having a CT-scan caused them to experience the same feelings. Mom knew we had to go through with this appointment because its sole purpose was to find out if the cancer had spread to other areas of her body.

The doctor decided to give her some anxiety medication to help during this appointment. They sent her into the waiting area with me for a while in order to allow the medication to take effect by calming and relaxing her enough to go through with the procedure. I remember her grabbing my hand in the waiting room, almost like she was a child again, saying, "I'm afraid Liza, I'm afraid."

"I know you are, Mommy, but you know that we must go through with this to help us find out what we are up against," I said softly. Finally, she began to relax, and as they called her back into the CT area, I could see the resignation in her face. She had to face this head-on, otherwise we would not be equipped to fight this battle in having the information that we needed concerning her body.

She emerged about forty minutes later and walked up to me saying with a deep sigh, "I did it, I did it." We were told at the reception area that the results would be sent to my mother's primary care physician and the physician would contact us with them in a day or two. As we drove home from the appointment, I could see my mother was already drained from her illness which I was beginning to recognize from the research that I had done, coupled with the fact that going through the CT-scan caused her increased anxiety. Witnessing all of this only confirmed for me the battle that we were in, and that I was not a bystander. I was a soldier in this battle caring for and carrying one of the wounded through the battlefield to a place of shelter.

The phone call from my mom's primary physician came within a few days as promised. We were asked to come in to see her for an appointment on the following day. As we drove to the appointment, I saw the same look on my mother's face as before: a wild-eyed look of fear, waiting to see where the next punch was going to come from, like someone caught in a fight blind and the punches were coming from everywhere. As I clenched the steering wheel of the car, I reassured myself in my mind that God had control of the situation and that He would give us what we needed to get through this.

We checked in at the reception desk for the appointment and sat for only a few moments. The nurse came out to escort us to the examination room, but this time took no vital signs. Since taking vital signs was the first action in coming into the examining room for any doctor's appointment, I was not sure if it were comforting or alarming.

As usual, the doctor knocked before entering the room once again. As the door opened she tried to make her face undetectable, but I recognized that same look of despair that we saw before.

"It is time to make a referral," she said. "They were unable to get the full results of the CT-scan because your mother had such difficulty with the machinery. However, they did get enough to confirm that she does indeed have lung cancer, and needs to begin some form of treatment immediately." Whether it would be surgically or through medication, she could not say. She needed for us to see someone with a level of expertise beyond hers in this particular area. We were then given an appointment to meet with a team of doctors who specialized in the treatment of lung cancer. I knew at this point, I would need to sit down with my boss and let her know what was going on and what I expected the future to look like as it related to my absence from work. I knew she would be understanding, as this was her nature, but also because her significant other's mother had died of breast cancer, so she had seen first-hand what a loved one and advocate would face in this situation. Needless to say, when we discussed my situation, she was extremely supportive and encouraging.

I worked a half-day on the day of the appointment with the medical team that would be working with us through this phase of my mother's diagnosis and treatment. I left work and headed home to pick up Mom for the appointment. She felt a little anxious, which was normal for someone facing cancer treatment. The doctor who had prescribed the anxiety pills told her that she could take them when needed. The prescription was not strong, so that she could take two at a time if necessary. We decided that she would take one at this point prior to the appointment, knowing the effects of medication can vary from person to person.

I find it interesting when I begin to look back on how I began to feel the role reversal in our relationship as Mom consulted me for everything, and I began to and needed to take charge of more of her life. I loved Mom with all of my heart as she loved me, her eldest child. However, she always had a strong personality, which my sister seemed to escape by being married and leaving the state.

Whereas I remained single, a single parent in my thirties, my mother still had a need to control, which caused much of the strife for years prior to her illness. I disliked the way she needed to control, but that was her way of loving, at least prior to accepting Christ and beginning to grow and mature in Him.

By the time we got to the appointment with the medical team, the anxiety pill had taken effect and Mom was much calmer than when we left the house. It was a bit strange to be called in a room where there were five to six doctors waiting for us. We found them to be full of compassion and caring, and it was such a comfort to us during this time. Although we knew they saw cases like this daily, we were not made to feel like they had become desensitized because these types of appointments were all too familiar to them. They opened with introductions and con-firmed what we already knew. Then they gave us some options and recommendations concerning my mother's present condition. The first option was sur-gery; however, they, as a team did not recommend this. What they explained was they could surgically remove the tumor from my mother's lung, however, because the tumor was about the size of a softball, it would literally take half of her lung. This would diminish her lung capacity severely, affecting her quality of life. The flipside of surgery was that it would ensure that they got it all from the lung, but what about other areas of her body?

What! I screeched in my own head, as I remained calm on the surface. "What do you mean other areas of her body"? I asked.

The doctor began to explain that cancer of the lung metastasizes to other areas of the body and can do it rapidly. One of the first areas is the brain, which had already begun in my mother's case. I heard the same gasp from my mother that I heard in the doctor's office the day of her diagnosis. Yes, this was another piece of gut-wrenching news we had to face. Now not only did my mother have cancer of the lung, but she had cancer in her brain. My thought was this appointment was scheduled to devise a treatment plan, not to give us more devastating news. As I tried to calm down, I heard my own words to my mother some days before regarding her CT-scan, "You know that we must go through with this to help us find out what we are up against." Well, indeed we had to hear this information so that we would know what we were dealing with and how to plan to defeat it. At this point, we decided as a team—the doctors, my mother, and me—to proceed initially with non-invasive procedures.

Our next scheduled appointment was with a female doctor who would explain the procedure that would be done to locate where the cancer was in her brain. The plan was to put her through an extensive series of radiation treatments. However, in order to successfully radiate the affected area, a special procedure had to be done that would be further explained by a brain specialist who would take over this portion of her treatment. Once the brain radiation treatments were complete, she would then go through several rounds of chemotherapy.

Chapter 4

THE JOURNEY: PHASE II

I felt like I had entered medical school as I searched the internet for information about lung cancer. The tears began to stream down my face. I was at work and things were not yet at a point where the general public was aware of my family situation. It was limited to those I reported to directly. Percentages of survival with lung cancer were low, especially with the inability to operate if the mass was too great in size, according to the statistical reports. There was so much research that I began to do. My nature is one of investigation and learning so I did what came naturally. I wanted to know—no, I needed to know—as much as the doctors did. Even though medicine was not my profession, I knew I had the ability to become a layman expert with the level of knowledge and information accessible to me on this subject.

My heart was weakened by all that I was learning about lung cancer, yet my faith would not. I knew the God that I served through His Son Jesus Christ could heal my mother of cancer, or anything else, as He had done before if and when He chose to. As long as she had breath in her body, she could be healed.

We had gone through the first phase of our journey and the second phase was about to begin. We were scheduled to meet with a world-renowned brain tumor specialist and his team in order for us to begin the brain radiation. The morning that we were scheduled for the appointment, Mom and I had another quiet ride to the hospital. Neither of us knew what to expect from this doctor and his team, or from the road ahead. I had spent time in prayer that morning as I normally did, then my mom and I before each appointment would spend a quick moment in prayer prior to getting out of the car. We had met so many people, so much factual information was presented, and lots of opinions that we knew especially for me as her advocate, that our minds had to be clear to make decisions— sometimes ones where there was not much time to ponder over them.

As we entered the waiting room of this famous brain specialist, there were many people there; in fact, the room buzzed with quiet chatter. I remember thinking this seemed like an ordinary clinic for patients with the flu. Yet, these people were all here to see the best of the best. My mother and I sat next to a woman who was quite friendly and full of information about the reputation of the doctor that we were there to see. In fact, all of these patients seemed to be there to see this one doctor who in their eyes had performed miracles. Although I too knew the history of the one that performed true miracles, I was thankful we had somehow landed upon the doorstep of a specialist in the field of brain tumors. On the other hand, should I have expected anything less or anyone less to be presented before us from a God that loves us so much?

Finally, we were called in for the appointment. The specialist that we were to see had a team of doctors that worked with him, and he was in surgery that morning. We met with a female member of his team who showed us the brain scan that had been done on Mom. As she talked, much of the research that I had been doing was confirmed by the information that she provided. She told us that the reason that Mom would need radiation treatment to her brain was because the way the brain was made, that it would not allow the chemotherapy drug to enter into that area of the body. I remember thinking at one point while she was explaining this phenomenon to us about the Scripture in the Bible, Psalm 139, that says *"I will praise thee; for I am fearfully and wonderfully made: marvelous are thy works; and that my soul knoweth right well."* To me, that meant we were made with such intricate detail that we were wonderfully complex, and that the workmanship of the one who made us is marvelous! They did not quite understand why the body reacted like this, but this was a fact and could not be changed. This meant the only effective and possible treatment would be radiation. It was decided by the doctor, my mother, and me that it was necessary to begin radiation to the brain as soon as possible. This meant within a matter of weeks. We knew the ability to think, intellectualize, and feel was housed in the brain. In addition, it is the controlling center of the nervous system and that because it regulated bodily activities, it would need to be dealt with first and foremost. Until this point, I had no idea what radiation to the body was or would do, or that chemotherapy was a drug. I realized I was in for a whole new level of learning through this experience with my mom, one that would change me forever.

Chapter 5

CANCER COLLEGE: A DIFFERENT KIND OF EDUCATION

We began the process of radiation treatments to Mom's brain. We had to go to a preliminary appointment, which would determine *exactly* where the brain needed the treatment. It was important that this be an exact science because radiation could cause damage to other areas of the brain. I spent time in prayer that morning, as usual, but there were times when it became difficult to pray. Not because I don't believe what or to whom I am praying, but because it became difficult to utter words; they didn't feel like enough. I did not lack faith, by any means. I knew the God that I served could heal my mother at any time, and that as long as she had breath, He could. The emotion that would come over me felt overwhelming at times, like I was in a movie. This could not be happening to us, to me—I could not have to make these kinds of decisions on my mother's behalf. Was I witnessing all that I was witnessing and about to witness?

We took a quieter than usual ride to the hospital today. I remember my prayer from this morning focusing more on God selecting the right people to perform this treatment, that there would be no error, and that everyone that should be there would be according to His hand-picked selection of specialists.

Once we arrived at the hospital, everyone was friendly, attentive, caring, and assuring. The staff that would be performing the procedure to pinpoint the area of my mother's brain that would be treated was introduced to us and we were told at that time what the procedure would entail and what each person would do. The team explained a device much like a halo would be secured to my mother's head, and that she would be anesthetized during this procedure. This halo would allow the machine to display my mother's brain in four quadrants so they could focus on each quadrant individually. After this startling explanation, they wheeled my mother off in a wheelchair to perform the initial part of the procedure.

I was left in a huge private waiting area and the only thing I could think to do and wanted to do the moment that the door closed was to pray. I was so filled with fear of the unknown, I needed comfort from my Heavenly Father. I needed to know the people that He had selected for us today were in place.

I began to pray in a way that yielded such power that I could feel the power of the prayer within me, a power that I had not felt before, nor did I expect to feel somewhere other than in the privacy of my home.

As soon as I had finished, there was a knock at the door. I responded after wiping away my tears, by telling the person to come in. It was the famous doctor that we had not yet had the privilege to meet until now. The one that everyone spoke of, even the staff when we got there that morning, told us how fortunate we were to get this particular man. He walked in with a smile that was warm and gentle, he spoke softly but confidently when he introduced himself.

"Your mother came through the attaching of the halo with success. She will arrive back in the room shortly, but please don't be alarmed by what you see. I will be back to speak with you both in a while. Things so far are going very well."

Finally, they rolled Mom back into the room. I remember gasping at first and then seeing that my mom had been crying. Her eyes welled up with tears as she said, almost like a child, "Liza, they hurt me." I fought back the tears as I looked at this huge monstrosity that they had drilled into my mother's skull! I felt for her, oh God how I felt for her. It looked painful and uncomfortable and they had to shave her head to draw on her head in order to map it so they would be sure of where they needed to radiate. It was heavy and I could see the screws! Once I got over the initial shock, and successfully fought back the tears, I comforted her and told her that her hair would grow back and said, "Well Mommy, at least they're not trying to make you disguise this as a hat for church on Sunday." We both laughed and it eased the pain.

Suddenly, there was a knock at the door, and the door opened to our doctor specialist entering with compassion on his face. He said to my mother immediately, "I know that you are uncomfortable but this is the only way to ensure that we hit the correct areas with radiation. I promise this part will be over soon." He then proceeded to explain the next part of the procedure which would be isolating the spots that needed to be radiated by using a map of the brain. They had neuro scientists on the team and other types of neurological specialists working on my mother's case. He sat in a chair as though we were guests at his home, offering us juice or water if we desired. He talked about himself and his own experiences that kept him working in this field. He talked about his family and his wife and children and grandchildren. He told us that his wife was the "minister" in the family; he talked about his salvation and the healing power of God. He asked us if we had any other questions that he could answer.

Finally, my mother interjected timidly with a final question, "Will you be with me through the rest of this procedure?"

His answer was so profound, he said, "Whither thou goest, I am with thee." With that, he smiled and left the room.

All I could do was close my eyes as the tears flowed and shake my head thinking about the awesomeness of a God who loves us so much that He would not only give us the best in this area of expertise, but someone who knew and believed in

Him. Even more than that, that He would answer my prayers so immediately. During my time of prayer in that very room, this was what I asked God for, that He would give us someone who knew Him and He did.

The ride home this time was filled with hope, gratitude, and the knowledge that God heard us, and He knew what we wanted before we did, but answered our prayer when we needed. How much more could we ask of a God whose love for us was so great? His faithfulness was all that we needed.

We received a phone call within forty-eight hours letting us know we were to start radiation treatments the following week. My mother would have radiation treatments to her brain once a week for the next twelve weeks.

I went back to work with a concrete work schedule to give to my manager, and had the ability to telecommute from home, so I used this option. It would keep me from using any family leave time or too much vacation time so soon since I did not know what was ahead.

We reported for our first day of radiation and the hospital staff was once again caring and pleasant to work with. I bless God that my mother and I had favor with the staff and they went out of their way each week to make us comfortable. There were a few times when I had to bring my daughter with us for the appointments. I usually waited in the waiting rooms, but when my daughter came, they allowed her to go into the play area with the children who had cancer and play with them. My daughter was a delight to the nurses and interacted so well with the children that they began to ask for her when she did not come with me to the appointments. I was so thankful that the appearance of the children many who were bald was not startling to my daughter. She asked, I explained, and she went on with little or no reaction to my explanation. She played computer games with them read to some of them and made a few friends in that twelve-week span of time. Each appointment was about an hour, so once I got my mother settled back at home, I would return to work for the day. This was not difficult for me and certainly not draining, although I began to see how tired my mother had become. There were no other visible physical differences; her hair grew back quickly, which we had prayed for, but she was exhausted as the treatments progressed. We got to a point when arriving at the hospital where I would have to let her out and get her to the lobby where she would wait until I parked the car, and I would come to meet her in the lobby. We would get the elevator to the treatment floor and the long walk down the corridors to the radiation area took forever. She walked slower and slower each week, weaker with each treatment. Watching her weaken took more out of me than the activity of getting her from location to location. It got to a point during the last weeks where I would automatically look for a wheelchair in the lobby because she could no longer walk the distance.

At the end of the twelve weeks, my mother could hardly get out of bed. It had been three months of radiation treatments every week. We had met many people who were regulars like we were, we rejoiced when some went into remission and would not return for radiation, and we cried when there were others that we would never see again.

The treatments to my mother's brain were successful, but they took their toll on other areas of her body and our lives.

We were allowed a four to five-week reprieve for my mother's body to adjust and rest before the next round of treatments began, chemotherapy. I had heard the word "chemotherapy" used so many times relating to cancer treatment, but had no idea what it was. I learned so much during this time of "Cancer College," which is what I coined it because it truly was a new and different kind of education.

Chapter 6

A DIFFERENT KIND OF EDUCATION: ROUND TWO

The first day of chemotherapy, reporting to the HMO that we as a family had been members of since I was sixteen years old, I never would have believed I would be going to the oncology area. But we were here, and ready for round two of treatments in hopes of extinguishing this enemy of my mother's good cells that had entered her body.

My mother felt much better after a five-week rest. She felt good, her hair had grown back beautifully and she had much more strength now than she did at the end of her round of radiation treatments. We did not quite know what to expect this time; however, I did acquire one major piece of education at the onset of this lengthy education. Chemotherapy—or at least, the type of chemotherapy drug that my mother would receive—would be administered intravenously. As we sat in the treatment room, we watched television. My mother was on a lounge chair and we were relaxed. We did not realize there was so much involved in my mother receiving this treatment. The medication, had to be ordered upon her arrival and sent down to the oncology area. Then the nurse had to come in and administer some pre-medications.

One of the pre-medications was a large dose of Benadryl to eliminate any problem that might arise from an allergic reaction to the chemotherapy. After receiving the Benadryl, my mom would get extremely sleepy and fall off to sleep. We would be in the middle of talking and before I knew it, I would hear a slight snore coming from her and she was knocked out. I was left to watch television in the room until the treatment was completed.

The treatments took about four hours, which meant I would not return to work on those days. I would use my time to telecommute from home and get my work done. I had been given quite a bit of literature from the hospital regarding the cancer drug and possible side effects. I read through all of it thoroughly and could have passed an exam on the subject. I kept such a close watch on my mother that the doctors depended upon me to notify them of anything different, any changes, and even some historical events that had occurred since the diagnosis and I knew them all. After about the third treatment, we came home on this particular afternoon and my mother was in an extreme amount of pain. Her legs hurt so badly that she was constantly screaming in pain. I called the hospital to let them know and they thought she might be having a reaction to the chemotherapy. They were going to have the primary doctor call me back before they would call in yet another prescription—one of many that she was already taking—however, this one was for the pain. They explained this may be a side effect of the chemotherapy that was uncommon to most recipients of that particular drug. All I could hear was my mom yelling my name and begging me to help her because she could not take the pain. She was rolling back and forth on her bed, screaming and crying. I began to panic and then cry because there was nothing that I knew to do.

"Mommy, please hold on. They're going to call me back, just please hold on," which did nothing to ease her pain. I began to pray and ask the Father, "Please, please help me. I don't know what to do." I wanted desperately to help her, but I just didn't know what to do. Suddenly, a thought came to my mind, one that I know had to be inspired by the Holy Spirit because there was no way that I, in my own thought process, could have ever come up with this idea. In addition, no doctor that I had encountered thus far would have ever told me to do precisely what the Father told me to do. I went to the towel cabinet in the house, and got a full-sized towel out of the closet. Went to the kitchen and wet the towel in the kitchen sink. Then I wrapped the towel up in Saran wrap and put it on a plate in the microwave for a few minutes to heat it. I went in to the bedroom where my mother was still screaming and said, "Mommy, hold on. I am bringing in something that I think will help. Just hold on."

Once the timer went off in the microwave, I waited about a minute for the towel to cool off. I could hardly take it out of the microwave, so I knew it would burn her if I immediately put it on her legs. I ran into the bedroom, put a pillow under her feet, and brought the hot towel in, still wrapped in Saran wrap and put it under her legs. What I heard made me almost break down and weep for joy. My mother immediately went quiet, and all that I heard was "Ahhhhh," with such a sigh of relief that it was humbling.

I had no responsibility in directing myself to make this non-medical decision other than to be obedient to the voice of the Holy Spirit. I was amazed at the results, but not so amazed not to believe and have faith that a Father that knows everything about us could not take something so simple and give it such healing power. We used this God prescribed, non-medical treatment each time my mother had leg pain after chemotherapy and it worked every time.

Chapter 7

THE JOURNEY: PHASE III

We were well into the fifth session of chemo-therapy treatments, and we had become adept at dealing with most of the minor complications that might arise from the chemotherapy. My mother was at the point where she was sick after her treatments, and her appetite had waned. I saw she had dropped weight and had little strength, especially after her treatments. I could once again see the toll the cancer treatment had taken on my mother's body and now on me. I had to help her walk to the bathroom constantly and she had gotten to a point where she could not raise herself off of the toilet once she had finished. I contacted the hospital patient liaison who placed an order for a raised seat for the toilet with bars on each side for her to pull herself up with. I would wait until she was finished and would get her back to the bed.

One morning, I received a phone call with my mother's frightened voice sobbing at the other end, "Liza, come here! Please come up here!"

I threw on a robe and went running up the backstairs to her house and found her sitting on the bed with all of her beautiful hair on her pillow. She had finally grown her hair back from the initial

shaving of it in preparation for the radiation treatments and now she had reached the point in chemotherapy that most people dread—the point that
can affect their self-esteem, their attitude, and
their life. My mother had shoulder-length hair that
she took pride in, and it was now gone, overnight!
She went to bed with a head full and woke up
to hair on her head that was about an inch long
in length and a few strands here and there that
were still shoulder length. I immediately gave her a
scarf to put on her head and said, "Mommy, I'm so
sorry." We knew this could happen because we had
read about it in the side effects; however, you never
know the effect of something like this happening
and certainly never feel the shock until it happens.

I remember Mom's biggest concern about
what she looked like now was the reaction of my
daughter. Alex was her Naunie's joy and she did not
want anything to upset or scare her. This thought
brought me back to when and how Alex found out
that my mother had cancer. I remember prior to
my mother's diagnosis that Alex came home with
a book from her school library about a mom who
had two daughters and the mom had cancer. In
retrospect, I wonder whether this was God's way of
preparing my child for what we would go through
as a family. I chose not to tell her about her Naunie
having cancer at the beginning because I did not
know how to approach the subject and I did not
want to scare her. I explained to her after her many
questions that Naunie was going to the doctor so
much because they were trying to take care of a
medical problem that Naunie had. To the inquiring

mind of a ten-year-old, this was not enough information, but she took it for the time being.

One evening, when she and I were in the car, Alex asked, "Mommy, does Naunie have cancer?" She asked this question calmly and matter-of-factly.

I paused, took a deep breath, and said, "Yes, Naunie has cancer." Thank goodness I was already parked or I think that I may have lost control of the car. "Why do you think she has cancer?"

"I just know, Mommy. Is Naunie going to be like the mother in the book that I took out of the library?"

"Well, what happened to the mother in the book, Sweetie?"

"The mother died, Mommy."

I told her that I did not think that and believed God would heal her for us. From that point on, we needed only give Alex explanations for a ten-year-old, but we did not hide anything from her.

With my mother having this fear of her granddaughter being afraid of her with no hair, I suggested to my mother that we show her Naunie's head, and even let Alex pick out cool scarves for Naunie to wear to decorate her head. My mother thought that this was a good plan and decided to share the news with my daughter that same afternoon. Alex arrived at the same time every day after school and she went directly up to my mother's house. Naunie had the scarf on as we decided she would and I decided to allow my mother to handle this news with Alex in her own way as a grandmother. They had a special bond, and I did not feel the need to interfere with how this explanation would take place. I trusted my mother's judgment and wanted her to feel free to give Alex the news independent of me.

After about an hour I could hear Alex's small footsteps coming down the back stairs of our two-family home as I was in the kitchen preparing dinner. The back door swung open and my child entered in wildly, yelling, "Mommy! Mommy! Did you see Naunie's hair? It's all gone!"

"I know, honey. I saw. Did it bother you to see her with no hair?"

"Well at first, because she told me she had something to show me and I got scared because I didn't know what it was. But then, she took off her scarf and let me rub her head and asked me if I was okay with seeing it. I told her yes, because no matter what, she is still Naunie, and I love her."

As my eyes welled up with tears, I realized how unconditional the love of a child really is, and how much our Heavenly Father wants us to love and trust Him equally as much.

My mother was at a point where eating a true meal for her was a bonus for both of us. It was so difficult to see this woman that once had such a healthy appetite not able to eat, not that she did not have the desire or get hungry; she either could not hold down the food, or her appetite was not there. This of course was one of the effects of the chemotherapy. However, as I finished preparing dinner, I fixed a small plate and brought it to her anyway, in hopes that she might be able to at least eat a spoonful or two. I had been praying about solutions for many of the obstacles that we faced during my mother's treatment. I had experienced the miraculous power of the Lord move on her behalf with the pain in her legs after her initial sessions of chemotherapy and He instructed me in what to do to dissolve her pain. I looked to Him for my strength, guidance, knowledge, understanding, and wisdom while we underwent this experience with surmounting grace.

Chapter 8

A YEAR TO REMEMBER

My mom's sixtieth birthday was approaching and I was filled with mixed emotions. I was so sorry that she had to go through a birthday with this illness and needing chemotherapy, but I was glad to see that she was in good spirits while approaching this day. My sister had planned to come home from Alabama to spend the time with my mom and me. She had not seen us since Christmas, and I desperately needed some relief at this point. I always found it interesting while going through this experience that when I did not think that I could handle another moment, the Lord would send relief, either by way of my sister making the long trip from Alabama to Boston for a week or so, or by putting my mother's closest friend in place, to just watch over her, while I got some much-needed rest, both physically and mentally.

My sister and I were excited about her coming home to Boston. I felt that I needed to prepare her in the best way possible for what she was about to see. I had had the privilege of seeing my mother gradually get to this stage of her illness, where she was totally bald, weak, constantly vomiting, and basically helpless. My sister, on the other hand, being far away, had not seen or experienced any of this, and had no idea what she was in for upon her arrival. As much as I tried to prepare her gently, nothing could have prepared her for this birthday experience with our mom.

As we talked together on the phone weekly prior to her arrival, she was bubbly and full of energy, which is her nature. She was filled with ideas about how we would spend this momentous occasion that I felt guilty at some points discouraging some of the ideas because I was here with the reality, which she had not yet seen. We talked about a party, which I flatly discouraged. We talked about going out to a fancy restaurant, which again I discouraged. As I listened to my sister's excitement wane, I realized she sounded somewhat hurt that I was not in favor of her great ideas. They were indeed great, but not practical for the stage that mom was in with her treatment.

We decided to table those ideas and to plan to have a dinner with her closest friends, something quiet, but one that would honor mom, and her friendships. So, we got together a list of eight of her closest friends, those that could handle the way she looked, and the fact that she was so ill. My sister took the list and began to make the phone calls. Even though it was long distance, it was a way that she could help in the planning and be a comfort to me being so far away, which I greatly appreciated. Everyone had agreed to attend, and my sister and I decided to cook a wonderful meal for all who were in attendance. We began to plan our menu within the next few days, since my sister would be arriving at the end of the week. We wanted to shop together for the dinner so the plan was to wait until she arrived for anything to do with the birthday dinner.

It was finally Thursday, the day that my sister would arrive. As I prepared to leave the house to pick her up from the airport, the reality hit me that we had experienced everything by phone. Now we would be going through all of this in person, together. I was scared for her. I can only imagine that she felt the same way, not knowing what she was about to witness. As I waited for her at the baggage claim, my anticipation began to build. My sister, my only sibling, was coming home, and I needed her. I felt alone most of the time throughout this experience, and when I could share any of it with her personally, it made such a difference for me. As she came through the airport I could see the look of excitement on her face my face lit up when I saw her. I can only imagine I may have looked a little tired and worn, but she was kind and did not mention it. Her first question was, "How's Mommy?"

"She's okay this morning; no sickness yet, but she is extremely weak and not sure how you will handle seeing her."

My mother was sincerely worried about my sister seeing her in this condition. I assured both my sister and mother that it would take a little getting used to but once the initial shock was over they both would be fine.

As we arrived in front of the house, my sister took in a deep breath. We decided to go directly up to my mother's house using my mother's front door instead of going through my house and using the back stairs. I took my key out and opened the lock, yelled to my mother that it was Shellie and I on our way upstairs. I went first to give my sister another moment to gather her composure, for as soon as we hit the top of the stairs, my mother's room was right there to the right. We carried the luggage with us since my sister would stay upstairs with my mom during her visit.

As my sister hit the top stair and turned the corner to the room, I saw the look on her face immediately. She was in shock, but tried not to show it. My mother was bald, had lost quite a bit of weight, and was extremely weak. This was not the woman that she knew. This was not Mommy! Shellie walked over to my mother's bed, hugged and kissed her, and laid next to her on the bed. My sister was famous for doing that. She, even in her thirties, married with a child, could come home and lay in the bed with Mom like she was seven all over again. I marveled at her ability to be like that with mom. I left them as they laid and talked. I knew my mom would need something in her system at this point, so I proceeded to the kitchen to make the God-inspired drink that I began to make for my mother with her inability to eat solid foods without getting sick. I got a can of frozen juice, usually orange, which I poured into a blender. I added a can of water, then cut up fresh bananas, kiwi, strawberries, peaches, and any other fresh fruit that I could get my hands on and thought would mix well. I blended it together and we had an amazing frozen drink, which she loved, since it was cold, fruity, filling, and did not make her throw up. As I brought it into the room, she immediately got excited and said, "Hmmm, Shellie, you've got to try this. You want some?"

"No thanks, Mommy. Maybe later."

At that point, I promised my sister I would show her how to make it since she would be here helping and staying upstairs.

After a few hours of reuniting between my sister and my mom, she and I decided we needed to go shopping for the food for the birthday dinner since it was in a few days. We went to the market and purchased Cornish hens, and our plan was to stuff them with wild rice and have broccoli. We also purchased ingredients for fresh salad, dinner rolls, and sparkling cider to toast with. We made sure there was coffee and tea in the house and we ordered a wonderful strawberry cake from one of the best bakeries in Boston for her birthday cake.

As much as I wanted to be excited about this upcoming celebration, it was difficult because I knew in reality how my mother might be feeling, having just gone through a round of chemotherapy. She was tough, but anyone going through this experience knows that there is no guarantee as to how you could feel within twenty-four hours of a treatment.

The evening of the dinner had finally arrived. Shellie and I busied ourselves with straightening up my mom's house and preparing for the festivities for the evening. Mom, as I had expected, felt lousy and was too weak to get out of the bed. We wanted her to rest as much during the day so that when the evening approached, she might have enough energy to at least sit and be entertained by her guests, since she was clearly unable to entertain them. These ladies were a group of her closest friends, so they would accept her any way and in any condition that she was in. They were humbled and honored to be spending this birthday with her, especially when she was battling for her life.

It was nearing 4:00 p.m. and the dinner was at 6:00, so Shellie and I began to prepare the food and set the dining room table for the guests. We had already prepared some light hors devours. Shellie went upstairs to begin to help mom get her face made up and put something on. She was quickly hit with the harsh reality of mom's condition as she tried to assist her. Mom was barely able to rise out of the bed and was vomiting from the chemo. Shellie knew Mom's condition, but it was so different to hear about all that was going on from a distance by phone. So she heard, but did not truly experience it all until now. I was in the kitchen taking the Cornish hens out of the oven and it was close to our guest's arrival time when my sister entered my back door from upstairs. I could tell by the look on her face that this experience had brought her to the breaking point. She began by moving quickly in the kitchen, helping me put the last things in the oven, and I so clearly remember that as she bent over the oven, the tears began to stream. She began to sob, and shake her head. She had not realized the magnitude nor depth of what we experienced. Not that she ever made light of it, but moreover, the fact that she was not dealing with this day in and day out. She had not seen my mom in about six months and so much had changed in that time. I did not know which was the worse of the two experiences: to be me, dealing and experiencing all of it on a daily basis, or to have not been there in such a long time like my sister, and to come in and see the deterioration and have it affect my sister so deeply. I felt for her at that point, more than for myself; her pain was so deep. I had the advantage and disadvantage of seeing and experiencing every change that my mother went through so that I needed no preparation when her condition deteriorated because I experienced it in stages. Unfortunately, my sister experienced it in one big blow. I was quiet, as my eyes welled up and filled with tears. I did not know what to say to even bring a small level of comfort to my sister. Not that I did not want to, but what could I say that would make this all better? What could I say that would make this situation change? "Don't worry"? "It will be all right"? "I understand how you feel"? None of the statements of comfort would be fitting in this situation. How was it that I, who had been dealing with this enemy called cancer, who had attacked our family and my mother—how was it that I could find no words, nothing that would be of comfort to her? Well, there was nothing comforting about this situation, nothing at all.

My mother had said to my sister that she could not do it today. She could not make it to see her friends. She was too weak and needed to stay in bed. My sister pleaded for a short time with my mother, who gave every effort to rise up, get dressed, and have her face made up, and finally realized this—at least for today—was an impossible feat. After we resolved that this was not going to change for my mother, we shifted into another gear. Shellie and I washed our tear-stained faces, hugged each other, and began to bring the rolls and salad up to the dining area where the women awaited this wonderful meal and time of fellowship. We announced to them in an apologetic tone that mom did not have the strength to sit at the table for the evening, but she wanted them to enjoy themselves. With such love and compassion, they understood and moreover made the decision to join her prior to the meal and after at her bedside in her bedroom, if acceptable to us and to her. We would not dare deny them the opportunity to help my mother celebrate her birthday, which could be her last with her closest and most loving friends around her.

They brought chairs and filled her room with the laughter and love of friendship, and a sisterly bond that could not be broken. My sister and I marveled at the simplicity of the evening. We served the women each course of the meal and amazing strawberry truffle cake for dessert. They were honored to be a part of this celebration of life and thanked us for making them a part of it. As we neared the end of the evening, a smile came across Mom's face, one of gratitude and joy for making the best of this sixty years of life for her. My sister and I were grateful to have had the opportunity to make this happen together. As the ladies began to exit for the evening, they hugged and kissed my mom, hugged and kissed each other, and respected the love and pain that they felt as they walked away from this special year to remember.

My sister was scheduled to leave in a few days, but wanted to be as much of a help as possible while she was there. I had realized how much the Lord was concerned about me during this time of caring for my mother. There were many times when I felt like I could not go on, and God continually placed people of such value in my life at the times when I needed the help the most. It seemed as though when I was at the end of my rope, He would allow my sister to come to Boston, and clearly I could not have made it through this birthday celebration or some of the other weekly appointments without her help, for I was truly at a point of weariness. It was also my desire for her to feel as much of part of the love and care for Mom as possible because I knew how difficult it was for her to travel back and forth to Boston from Alabama, both financially and emotionally.

With the few days that we had left for Shellie to spend with Mom, we also had regularly scheduled chemotherapy appointments that she had not yet experienced. The last appointment prior to my mother's birthday had been two weeks before and this was a brand new week. We had also scheduled in advance an appointment with the doctor so that my sister could be present to hear some of the details of my mother's progress. As we drove to the chemotherapy appointment, my mother was in good spirits. Tired, but in good spirits, still feeling the joy of being surrounded by her friends and her two daughters, which did not happen often, since my sister had moved to Alabama. I dropped Shellie and mom at the front door and went to park the car. I did not realize how much I could appreciate just having someone to help me get mom out of the car closer to the destination so that she did not tire so easily. We had obtained handicapped tags, but there was still sometimes a distance between the handicapped parking and the front door of any given location. Yet, I could not always just let her out of the car in front of a location while I went to find a parking space for fear that she could fall with little to no strength some days. So, having my sister as another set of hands and feet was truly a blessing.

I met them in the clinic area waiting room and we sat and laughed with each other as we waited for the long day ahead. My sister and I always had the ability to laugh and to make one another laugh, even in the worst times of adversity. It was part of our way of bonding and our determination not to allow the adversity to completely take our joy. As they called us into the room and ordered the chemo cocktail for my mom, all the prep work had to be done. Shell was amazed at how much prep work it took in order for Mom to have this treatment. She watched and listened intently as steps were taken to ensure accuracy with this procedure. Mom dropped off to sleep pretty quickly from the Benadryl, which my sister did not expect. I forgot to mention this would happen during the three hours that we would be there. We talked as my mother's treatment took place. We even shared how it was hard to believe this was a part of our reality right now—that we were here, with our mother, having chemotherapy treatments for lung cancer. Something about the reality of those moments did not feel real. I gave Shellie an idea of what to expect when we got back home in regards to the condition that Mom would be in, but without experiencing it, it is hard to imagine.

Once the chemotherapy session was finally over, we were able to go home. Mom would always end up hungry, or at least *think* she was after the sessions. Admittedly, I did notice a change or increase in her appetite, but only at the beginning due in part to a prescribed medication that contained steroids. However, the increase was not real; it was almost like a false sense of hunger. Nevertheless, I would always get so excited as I did this time when my mother asked for pizza. I dropped her and Shellie off at the house while I picked up a pizza. Mom wanted the works on it, and I wanted her to have whatever she wanted. I gave Shellie instructions on what to do when we got Mom home, with any leg pain, which included using the natural prescription that the Lord had given me for her leg pain that I had used since her first chemotherapy session. She looked forward to this therapy as it had continued to work and brought her a great sense of relief.

I had arrived home with the pizza with excitement and fixed Mommy a plate, only to be deflated by the fact that her eyes were much bigger than her stomach, and by evening, she might be too sick to eat anything. Once again, Shellie took her spot on Mommy's bed and laid and talked with her. This was the routine after arriving home from each chemotherapy session with the exception of having my sister there, which I truly longed for. She would leave in a few days, but for now, I wanted to expose her to as much as possible in order to maintain her sense of involvement with everything happening during Mom's illness.

Mom had a fairly good night, and slept through most of it. Normally, I would go up and check on her first thing in the morning, but my sister was there, which gave me an opportunity to lay in bed for a few extra minutes before it was time to give her the meds that she needed for the morning. My mother knew Shellie would be leaving the next day and wanted to spend as much time as possible with her while she was still here, so I left them to their time together.

I was glad my sister had come for Mom's birthday. Not only to celebrate her birthday, but to give me some relief. The Lord sent her to Boston to back me up, cheer me up, and enable her to play an integral part of what our family was going through.

As we drove to the airport, there was silence and sadness. I hated for her to go. I needed her to be here with me, not living over a thousand miles away. We arrived at the airport with plenty of time to spare, and to talk before she got on her flight.

I promised I would constantly keep her updated as to Mom's progress. I remember getting back into the car after she boarded her plane and crying because I did not want to go back and face my life's reality alone. Nevertheless, it was indeed my reality and I had no choice but to face it.

Chapter 9

THE JOY OF REMISSION

All of the treatments had finally come to an end: no radiation, no chemotherapy, and few medications to take. Everything had come to a screeching halt, including what appeared to be the spread and symptoms of the cancer. Mom began to look and feel wonderful. She attended church services again, which made her feel so much better. Although during her treatments she tried as much as possible to get there, the treatments took too much out of her and she could barely get out of the bed half of the time. But this was a wonderful time, and I saw such joy in my mother as she dressed each Sunday for church and listened to her gospel music so that my ceilings would almost rattle. But it did not matter; she had true joy and I marveled at what she experienced and felt.

The winter months were upon us and New England winters are known to be quite treacherous. But this did not discourage my mother from desiring to return to her responsibilities as a missionary as the head of the missionary department at the church. She loved what she did and the people that she served with at church. They called her "Mother Deloatch", even though she was not typically the age of a mother of the church, she carried herself with the wisdom and nurturing that comes with the title of mother. Many young women would connect themselves to my mom, as though she was a surrogate mother for them. I never felt slighted with their affection for my mother, but I felt more honored that she had that kind of effect on them.

Mom had lost lots of weight from the cancer and the treatments, but never looked sickly. In fact, she was given compliments on a regular basis about how good she looked with the loss of weight and how spry she was. The pep in her step was back, and I was so grateful to see her that way. She was eating again—not as much as before, but she at least ate. We shopped together, and had the opportunity to spend some great times together, along with my daughter Alex.

During this time, her hair grew back and it was beautiful. She would have me put it in rollers for her every Saturday evening in preparation for church on Sunday morning. She was even driving back and forth to church on Sunday mornings for service. Since I had to be there much earlier for prayer, and as a Sunday school teacher, we thought it best not to tire her out by her being there all day. However, she did get to a point where she wanted to and did attend Sunday school as well.

I was also able to return to work during this time. I started back part-time so that I would be available for my mom which worked out perfectly for the whole family. Mom witnessed to more people than you could imagine during this time about the love of Jesus Christ. How much she loved Him, how much He loved her, and how much He loved us all. She had no fear about talking about her Lord and Savior to anyone who would listen, because she knew what He had brought her through. Mom wanted to experience everything during this time. She was like a kid who wanted to go everywhere and do everything. She realized that for the past year, she was imprisoned by this deadly disease that had threatened to take her life. She was now breaking free and she felt good; we felt good and life was fantastic!

Spring was finally coming and the flowers had begun to bloom and the weather was warmer. This of course meant Mom was even more anxious to get out and enjoy the days to come. We did exactly that—we shopped and went on day trips and did all that she had the energy to do. We began to plan for her upcoming birthday in May, Mother's Day, and summer barbecues, all of which she looked forward to with excitement.

We had a great spring together as a family and Mom celebrated her sixty-first birthday, which was not nearly as traumatic as her sixtieth. This one was a little quieter but certainly she felt better and we were all able to enjoy it. We enjoyed the spring months with many more outings. Mom loved to shop, especially since her weight loss, she wanted to look as good as she felt in her clothing. We had always enjoyed going to the stores together, even when my daughter was young. Now that my daughter was older, she could enjoy the experience with shopping with her Nauni and mommy and have many girl's days out.

Our summer was filled with food on the grill and warm summer days on the patio relaxing with friends and family. I did most of the cooking on the grill, especially when it came to grilling fish and seafood. As native New Englanders, fish and seafood were part of the main staple of our family diet. We cooked and enjoyed eating it year around, especially at summer time. We had much laughter and fun times during this time of remission that we as a family experienced together. I remember having such a blissful feeling that we had made it through. Doctor's reports were positive: no spreading of the cancer and everything appeared stable. Although I was a little nervous with her driving, my mother was back to driving her little green Subaru on a consistent basis. She drove distances that were not too far from home, but certainly she had a feeling of independence again which I believe contributed to her being in such high spirits. Mom always had such a great sense of humor; I remember we had to get her some fairly thick glasses to improve her eyesight. At the time she was still taking a medication that contained steroids, but it had begun to cause her some problems with her sugar levels, ultimately developing into diabetes. One of the effects began to manifest itself in her eyesight, which we were able to remedy after checking with the doctor. We found non-prescription glasses that she was able to use to improve her vision. I remember as we got into the cooler months where it got dark earlier, I began to do more of the driving after dark. Mom was not as comfortable with night driving, especially wearing glasses that were as thick as Coke bottles. We laughed about it all the time, especially when she would ask me jokingly after we had had a long day of shopping and I appeared to be tired of driving, "Do you want me to drive?" We found such humor knowing that we could not dare put her behind the wheel after dark.

One evening while driving home and it was nearing the holiday season, Mom and I were alone in the car. We were chatting as usual, and as I drove down a busy street where we were stopped in traffic, Mom exclaimed, "Look at all of the millions of beautiful Christmas lights!" I stopped talking and immediately thought to myself, *millions of Christmas lights! What Christmas lights?* I then asked her calmly but nervously about her observation.

"Mommy, where are the millions of Christmas lights that you see?" There were a few decorations on this main street, but millions? Absolutely not!

As she pointed ahead, she said, "Right there in front of us. See them? They're white and red," as though I should be seeing what she saw. I realized what my mother saw as Christmas lights were the brake lights of all of the cars in front of us in traffic. I chuckled at the cute innocence of my mom and sweetly replied, "Mommy, those are not Christmas lights. You are so cute. Those are the brake lights of the cars."

She let out a howl of laughter until I began to laugh. It was contagious as we could always find humor in something. She said to me laughingly, "Well, since I can see the lights so brightly maybe, I should drive home."

I responded, "Sure I'll pull over in just a minute and let you take over the wheel." We both laughed and I continued on our journey home.

Chapter 10

THE GIFT OF FORGIVENESS: THE LAST CHRISTMAS

It was December, and we had been blessed with six months of remission for Mom and a beautiful holiday season. She was still as spry as ever, planning the upcoming Christmas holiday and the New Year. We had a fun-filled Thanksgiving with some friends from church and my sister, brother-in-law, nephew, and cousins, where we ate fellowshipped played games and had lots of laughs. Mom was so delighted with being able to fill her home with noise and laughter during the holiday season.

A few weeks after the Thanksgiving festivities ended, Mom and I were in her kitchen discussing possibilities for Christmas. She looked at me seriously now and said, "I want to spend Christmas with your dad and stepmother." My mouth dropped open at her request, not believing she was serious. But indeed she was—she wanted to have dinner with them, which would include my stepfather, my daughter, and me going to my father's house.

I did not quite understand her request, but I was in the habit at this point of giving her anything that she wanted. I realized how valuable any request that she made was no matter how difficult or unusual it might be. She wanted it, and I made it happen. I did not know how long I had with her and wanted to fulfill as many of her wishes as I could.

"I'll call dad to ask him and will let you know what he says."

The relationship that my mother had with my father now was stable since my father had been remarried now for over thirty years. In addition, my sister and I had a good relationship with my dad and my daughter had a great relationship with her papa and her nana, which is what she called my stepmom. My stepmom was always kind and loving and her children and my sister and I always got along fantastically. We were a blended family that showed true love for one another. Daddy and Nita always attended every school and church function that my daughter was a part of, along with my mom and stepfather. In thinking about the upcoming holiday, it would be no different than one of those events, other than the fact that there would be other family members and friends in attendance.

I had been praying about how to approach the subject of our invasion on Christmas for dinner. I did not fear his response, but was seeking the Lord as to how to answer any questions that might arise from my father as to my mother's reasoning for making this request. Also, I needed to know how to go back to my mother with any negative response that I might be given by the request. Although my parents were now experiencing stability in their relationship with each other, this was not always the case. My mother vehemently resented my father for years as I believe that although my father did not openly state it, he too had a level of resentment for my mother.

My mom and dad were married at a fairly early age, as were most couples in their generation. They were married for thirteen years when things somewhere in the marriage just stopped. We were a broken family, my sister and I at the ages of eleven and six. The storms continued between my parents for many years after, through separation and divorce. It took many years until my sister and I, or at least I, had reached adulthood until my parents were tolerable with one another, especially my mother toward my father. Finally, once my daughter was born, there was something in common that they shared, grandparenthood. Even though my dad had remarried, and Nita was another wonderful grandma for my daughter, Dad and Mom shared the events, celebrations, school activities and everything else that happened around their granddaughter with mutual respect for their spouses, their daughters, and each other. As I grew in Christ, I became concerned about my mother's feelings toward my dad, even though I was at an age of understanding now. I never took sides, and always tried to see the story from both sides, but my mother was bitter and full of un-forgiveness for things that she felt my father could have handled differently during and after their divorce. Now, after all of these years of being full of bitterness, my mom wanted to have dinner at my dad's house for Christmas!

Dad and Nita knew in theory what I was going through with my mom, but neither of them could know what I was dealing with because I did not interact with them or talk about it with them on a daily basis. As I broached the subject with my dad on the phone, I said, "So I had a request from Mom to ask you about regarding the Christmas holiday."

There was silence for about thirty seconds and then, "Well, what is it?"

"Mom wants us to have Christmas dinner with you and Nita at your house this Christmas."

"You're kidding."

I could tell that there was a bit of discomfort with hearing this request. My father knew to some degree the feelings that my mother had toward him and he certainly had his own feelings toward her.

After another brief silence, he asked in a calm voice, "Any reason why she wants to have dinner here for the holiday?"

"I don't have a clue," which, at the time, was true.

"Well I have no problem with it, but I will check with my wife and let you know."

A few days went by and my dad called me to say we were welcome to come and have Christmas dinner with them and that I should bring my usual contribution: the baked macaroni and cheese. That was one of my specialties during the holiday season.

I was unable to fix it on a regular basis because you could use all of the allowable daily caloric intake for the average adult in one serving of this cheesy, rich tasting baked macaroni and cheese.

Christmas morning was finally here, and although I felt differently about this Christmas than I had in the past, I was thankful and full of joy that we were all here to see another Christmas holiday. Mom and I called my sister in Alabama to wish her my brother-in-law and my nephew a merry Christmas and talked with them for a while. We were not due to go to my dad's house until sometime after noon since dinner would be at 4:00. My mom had a chance to rest and relax before we went out for the day and we had a chance to open gifts with one another. Of course, her delight for the day was to watch her granddaughter open gifts on Christmas morning. Alex was never an early riser so we usually had to wait for her to wake up to open gifts unless I woke her up.

We began opening gifts around 10:00 and had a light breakfast to hold us over until dinner. I also knew that there would be snack foods at my dad's house so we would not suffer at any point during the day due to missed-meal cramps. At about 11:30, we began preparing ourselves with baths and getting dressed. I helped Mom get everything together then went downstairs and got my daughter bathed and dressed, sent her back upstairs with my mom, and finally got myself bathed and dressed.

I prepared most everything for the macaroni and cheese the night before and just had to slip it in the oven for about an hour. Once the macaroni and cheese was baked, we packed up and began on our journey to Dad and Nita's for the holiday dinner.

My dad and Nita lived about forty-five minutes North of Boston and this would be the first time my mother had been to their home where they had lived for at least twenty-five years. We had a good drive filled with Christmas spirit and my mom was exceptionally happy about this Christmas. As we pulled into the circular driveway at my dad's house, I had my daughter go in and let them know we were there while my stepfather and I helped my mother out of the car. By this time a few male family members were coming to grab bags with gifts and food and anything else that needed to be carried in. With my mother never having been to my dad's house, this was all foreign to her. She entered the front door and grabbed the banister to their split-level house and began to hoist herself up the stairs as I stood behind her to catch any missed steps. She did well upon entering the house; she was joyful and smiled and warm to all she met, as they were to her. My dad and Nita set a chair for her in the living room from the dining area so that she would not get stuck on the couch by sinking in if she needed to get up. She sat and conversed with everyone—no one would have believed this was the same woman that harbored such animosity.

However, I knew they still cared about each other's well-being. How could any couple that had been married to one another for many years and shared the joy of bearing children together not care about the other's well-being even through divorce?

Nita was her wonderfully sweet self, especially toward my mom, which was only natural for her, and made everyone feel welcomed and at home. My stepfather was the kind of person who never met a stranger, so he was just as at ease as everyone else and we all enjoyed each other's company. My aunt and uncle were there, from my dad's side and Nita's family members were there, including my stepsister and stepbrother and their spouses and children. The blend of our families was so unique that our children called each other cousins and called us "auntie" and "uncle" even though there was no blood relationship. This was all through the marriage of Dad and Nita. My mom and step-father blended in equally as well, as they usually did during Alex's events, but this time there were more people gathered together.

Dinner was about to be served and I was careful to watch over my mother as I always did as her caregiver. Making sure she had taken all of her medications and that she had light snacks before dinner in order for her to maintain her strength, especially during what would be such a long day for her. We all ate heartily during this holiday and shared so much love and family bonding time, that I was astounded by the experience. My mom had such a great time and everyone had a great time with her. I even think my dad enjoyed the interaction and was not dreading the fact that he had made the decision to comply with my mother's wishes.

It was getting late and I could see my mother's strength waning. Although she tried to hide it well,

I knew her every move at this point and it was time. I thanked my dad privately for honoring my mother's wishes, my mother thanked everyone for such a lovely time and we packed up and took the forty-five-minute drive back to Boston. As we pulled into the driveway at home, we followed our regular routine: my daughter took the keys to open my mother's door, and my stepfather and I got my mother out of the car and helped her up the steps. Nights like tonight were a bit difficult because my mother was tired and didn't have the strength to get up to the second floor of our duplex house where she lived. With patience on all parts, we got up there, I pulled the car into the driveway, and came up after parking the car to help her get ready for bed.

"Mom, did you have a good time?"

A soft smile came over her face as she closed her eyes and briefly nodded, "Yes baby, yes I did."

I knew something had happened and I was not sure what, but something had happened to my mother as a result of this experience. I got her into bed, kissed her, told her that I loved her and said I would see her in the morning. I remember going downstairs, putting my daughter to bed, and then retreating to my living room and into my favorite chair, the one that I always held my prayer sessions in. All I could tell my Heavenly Father was "thank you" as the tears rolled down my face because I knew what had happened. My mother had ended her battle with un-forgiveness and bitterness toward my dad. She had resolved with herself and with the Lord that she could no long harbor those feelings in her heart, but that she had to change. Her desire to share this Christmas with my dad and Nita had truly resulted in a gift of forgiveness. Not only did my father receive this gift which he may not have even been aware of, but surely my mother knew she too had received a gift for herself. She could now rest easy in her spirit and in her soul knowing that her Heavenly Father had forgiven her as well.

Chapter 11
A FIGHT TO THE FINISH: THE FINAL TEST

By 2001, we had not been in this battle for long, but it felt long based on our resources. We were indeed an army. A family coping, encouraging, praying, and hoping. Admittedly though, our adversary was powerful and difficult to ignore.

I could tell my mom was weary and the disease had started to take its toll. Due to one of her medications, she began to have elevated sugar levels that developed into diabetes. This was only realized when I went upstairs to her house after receiving an alarming phone call from her one Saturday afternoon.

She was walking around but said, "I'm really not feeling well today."

I sat in her room and asked her to describe her symptoms and the only visible symptom that she could describe was that her left hand kept jumping and shaking. I asked how long this had been going on and she stated it had been going on for most of the morning. By this time, it was mid-afternoon. I had spoken to her several times throughout the day, but this was the first mention of how she felt. I heard her music blasting as she usually did while praising the Lord, so I thought that everything was all right. I asked what it felt like when her hand was shaking as I could see no visible signs at that time. She said there was not pain, but she could not control it when it began to shake. As she described what it felt like, her hand began to shake and I saw what she was talking about. I was immediately concerned. She had never had anything like this before, but for some reason, I had a notion of what it might be.

In order not to alarm her, I went into the other room and called the doctor on call with our HMO. I explained to the nurse that it appeared as though she might be having a type of seizure but not one that would cause a person to fall out. I was familiar with seizures because my stepdad suffered from the worst kind and I knew many of the signs. The nurse took down my information and pulled her records and said she would have the doctor get back to me right away. The doctor got back to me within minutes and asked if he could review her files and call me back again. I said, "Yes, of course," and awaited the phone call. Upon his return phone call, he asked a series of questions, and I answered them and I then offered more information regarding frequency of this uncontrollable shaking that appeared to be getting worse. His suggestion was to get her to the nearest emergency room. He asked for our preference of hospital since there were a few excellent ones in the area, I told him our preference and he said he would call ahead.

My biggest fear with this situation was that I did not want my mother to fall out while trying to get her down the stairs or even in and out of the car. She was already dressed so we could leave immediately for the hospital, which was about fifteen minutes away.

As I pulled into the emergency lane of the hospital, my stepfather took her into the check-in desk. I was then able to park the car nearby by letting the parking attendants know I would be in the emergency room. By the time I entered the emergency room, my mother was in a wheelchair and the nurse was asking questions. I took over for my stepfather and began to answer the rest of the questions that the nurse was asking regarding my mother's current condition, including questions about her stage of cancer. Finally, they had us sit for a while in the emergency waiting area until we were called.

I was asked a series of questions again, which I answered and the doctors decided to take my mother's blood sugar level. The results had come back and her blood sugar level was well above 800. I gasped as I heard the number and the nurse and doctor looked at us and could not figure out how my mother had *walked* into the emergency room instead of being brought in by ambulance in a coma. They were in disbelief at what they saw the numbers to be in her test results. They immediately prescribed insulin and another type of medication. They equipped us with a prescription for a blood level monitor with test strips to pick up at the pharmacy immediately following my mother's release from the hospital.

As the emergency room doctor left, my mother had a pleasant surprise: it was her primary care physician whom we had not seen since her initial diagnosis. She was the on-call resident for our HMO at the hospital that afternoon. She greeted us with such warmth and made sure that my mother was comfortable and went over the charts, records, and test results to make sure she was informed as to all that had happened during our visit to the hospital. We were grateful to the Lord, whose timing is perfect. He made sure that in this emergency situation, we had the best care possible by people who knew our history. The hospital itself had a fine reputation; however, I found that in dealing with a few emergency situations while my mother had cancer, that when she as the patient went in to an emergency room environment, the medical staff did not know her history, which made it difficult for her and the doctors. I remember, during one emergency episode that we had, giving my mother's history to the emergency room doctors and then again to hospital residents at least three times.

I then told the final set of doctors that came in to see us and asked the same questions, in an agitated tone, "My story has not changed; I have recited the same answers to the same questions three times to each set of doctors that has entered this room, have the nine of you not had a conversation with one another to determine what information you have gathered as a group? I do not think that I need a medical degree to figure out that this would be the appropriate next course of action where your patient was concerned."

This was one of the reasons that it was always important for me to be present with my mother in dealing with any medical situation in her condition. It was difficult enough for her to be the person afflicted with this enemy of her body, but to be able to recount every medical detail was almost impossible, especially to have to recount it several times. I became the medical layman, historian, and decision maker regarding my mother's health during this entire battle with cancer.

Arriving home with my mother after this emergency visit to the hospital had my emotions high. I asked my mother if she wanted one of her favorite fruit drinks that I would fix her and she said she would take one later. She needed to rest after the hours spent at the hospital being poked and prodded. This break was good for me because it would give me some time to release my friend who so graciously cared for my daughter while I was gone and to spend some time in prayer once everyone was settled. I needed to relax in the presence of the Lord, to release all of the anxiety from the day, from the situation, and from my life at this point. I realized this new medical situation came with additional responsibility that I could unfortunately not leave in the hands of my stepfather. He had become so disjointed from all of this, so removed from the responsibility of it that he did not make any effort to take on any responsibility when it came to my mother's illness. Even during the times when I would wait to see if he would take the initiative to do something on his own, he would not and I would be called by my mother to assist her. I remember one night being called at around 2:00 a.m. by mom. The phone startled me, especially at this hour, because I thought the worst given my mother's condition. She was crying because she had to use the bathroom, my stepfather had taken up living out of the spare room in their home and although she continued to call for him, he either did not hear her, or chose not to respond. Either way, I rushed upstairs to assist my mother out of the bed, help her into the bathroom, and then to wait to lift her off of the toilet, clean her, and then get her back to bed. I remember the anger mixed with confusion that I felt, as I entered the spare room where my stepfather slept with the door open. At the time, it was inconceivable to me that he would not have been able to hear my mother's cries to him for help. Not only did this make me immediately feel a sense of resentment toward him, but I now feared that should any other real emergency situation arise, he would not respond and if she were unable to get to the telephone... I was afraid to think any further.

As I called his name a few times, he finally woke up. "Yes?"

"Did you hear Mom yelling for you for help?"

"No, I did not."

Well, I certainly could not accuse him of lying which was not my intention. "Please, you need to be more attentive to Mom, because I can't do this alone, especially calls in the middle of the night."

His response was one of silence, which caused me to turn and retreat from the room as quietly and quickly as possible in order not to allow my anger to build.

I had to realize my stepfather's way of dealing with this entire situation was not to deal with it. He did not volunteer to come to chemotherapy sessions, or radiation sessions, and I had to be careful because I knew my mother, in her own way, was protecting him from this, and I, on the other hand, did not want him protected. I felt he needed to be as involved as possible. He was her husband. However, in order not to upset my mother, I continued to take on all of the responsibility and the resentment began to build, not toward my mother, but toward my stepfather and their marriage.

There were many times that I had to remind him and make requests that he cook for my mother, and in some cases not just for Mom, but for the family since I was tied up with still trying to raise a child, work, and caring for my mother in his stead. His routine would be to get up for work at 4:30 a.m. and be out of the house around 5:30. He would arrive back home around 2:00 p.m. and come up the stairs, where my mother's bedroom was. One could either enter the dining room through French doors or take a left at the top of the stairs straight into her bedroom. He would enter through the bedroom, where, in most cases, I would be sitting with her. He would speak and walk straight through to the spare room. I understood how difficult this was for him and that everyone handles pain differently, but this was a family problem, not an individual one. Now my prayers had increased, not only for my mother's healing, and for the strength to carry out what God had given me to do, but also not to harbor resentment and un-forgiveness in my heart, which was a mounting effort.

My mother's condition was beginning to worsen. All of her treatments had ended months before and she was in remission. But there were signs leading to the fact that the cancer had become active again and possibly with a vengeance. My mother had terrible pain in her hip as she slept at night. She had come to a point where she was unable to sleep on her right side. Her walking was affected; although she could walk, there were times when it was painful. She was no longer driving on her own, and my stepfather could no longer drive due to his own medical condition, which left me to do all of the driving necessary for the family. This I handled with ease, compared to everything else. My mother's hip pain had intensified and I could see it on her face, even though she hid it well. I knew her stoic nature well enough to know when she was in real pain. I called the doctor and made an appointment for her to be seen. The doctors immediately responded and set her up for an appointment within two days. As we drove to the doctor's office, we did our usual chatting, but my mother was a bit quieter than usual. I asked her what was wrong and she replied that she was concerned about the hip pain, and hoped that the doctors could render her some immediate relief. The doctor checked my mother's hip and sent us down for an X-ray. To our surprise, he then suggested that she be set up for an MRI. I was concerned by the suggestion of such an extreme test, but we had worked with these doctors for over a year now and along with our relationship with God, the Master Physician, for the most part, we trusted their medical judgment. The doctor gave me the referral information that I needed to make the appointment for the MRI prior to us leaving the office. He stated that once the test was done and they had the results, he would call to schedule a follow-up appointment with him. We left and the ride home was quiet.

I tried to lighten up the atmosphere by talking about how we should appreciate how consistently thorough they always were, and how, after working with us for such a long time, they trusted our judgment enough to take us seriously and act immediately when a phone call came in. My mother agreed quietly but I could see that she was worried. I was not sure if she was worried about the test or worried about the results. Once again, this type of machine had the patient enclosed, and my mother had not forgotten her experience with the initial CT-scan. I promised I would do some research prior to and during the discussions with the MRI place, which had been my *modus operandi* throughout her illness.

As we arrived back at the house, my plan was to go back to the office. I was now on a part-time status again, since the recent changes in my mother's health. The changes were not enough for me to take full family leave yet, for which I was grateful to the Lord, however, from time to time, my status had changed from full-time with the combination of working from home now to part-time. My company had been wonderful in accommodating our family during this difficult time.

I returned to my office and proceeded to check email, voicemail, and respond to all necessary requests. That took the first hour of my afternoon, after which time I called my sister to let her know of Mom's appointment, the results, and the plan.

"I'll let you know once the appointment is made."

"Thanks, I appreciate that you always keep me informed of everything that you do with Mom."

I then began to do some research on the internet about the MRI exams. I found there were two types and both yielded the same results. One was an open MRI and the other closed. The difference was the type of machinery in that the closed one enclosed the patient into a tube, almost like the CT-scan that my mother had previously experienced and would not be able to handle at this juncture. The other was an open MRI, where the machine would encircle the patient instead of completely enclosing them and sending them into a tube. As I called to make the appointment, I asked the referral department if there were any places that had an open MRI close to us. She mentioned a place about a half-hour away from our home, which was perfect. I accepted the date that she provided, which was about a week away, with the prior knowledge that, if needed, I could use vacation or sick time for that day.

The day had arrived for the MRI and we would be headed out once again for a major medical procedure. I could feel the tension that my mother felt as we spoke on this particular morning. I wondered if she knew more than I and was not sharing or if she was nervous about the procedure. I asked her what was going on with her, and she shared she was nervous about this machine because it was unfamiliar. She clearly remembered the experience with the CT-scan and could not get that experience out of her head. I assured her that they said "open", and when they said "open", they meant *open*. I was able to make a late afternoon appointment for us. I could work in the morning until about lunchtime then go pick up my mother and drive to the appointment. I left work as planned, and called ahead to make sure my mother was ready so I would be prepared for any extra help she might need prior to leaving the house. She was all set and ready to go with the exception of coming down the stairs on her own. I knew that I would need to assist her with the trip to the car, which I would always allow time for. As we pulled up to the location of the MRI center, we prayed in the car and proceeded to enter the building.

As always, we were greeted with warmth and kindness by the entire staff, which always made the experience easier. We were directed to a room where my mother needed to change into a hospital gown and remove jewelry in order to prepare for the MRI. At one point my mother appeared so tense that I thought she would burst into tears.

I touched the small of her back and said, "Mommy, I will be here every step of the way, including in the room when they do the MRI. You'll be fine, so stop getting yourself so worked up, okay?" I said all of that as softly yet firmly as possible without making her feel as though I was being insensitive to her feelings, especially because I was not the one having to go into this machine.

As we sat in the waiting area after putting my mother's clothing into the assigned locker in the changing area, we talked about my having con-tacted my sister and her response. As usual, I assured my mom that I would contact my sister with any news. After about a ten-minute wait, the technician came to get us to escort us into the room with the MRI machine. Mommy walked so slowly behind us. I kept looking back to make sure she was okay. I was not sure if she walked so slowly because of the pain in her hip, or more because of the hesitation she had about this machine. We finally made it into the room where a huge machine took up almost the entire square footage of the room. We had been given the choice of bringing some music with us, which we did. I grabbed a worship CD out of the car just before entering the building and I was glad that I did. The machine itself was overwhelming to look at, and as much as it was indeed not a tube, I could see the effect that its mere size had on my mother.

The technicians helped Mom up onto the table of the machine and laid her down. Her head was to remain still, and they secured her head in some light restraints in order for her to keep it in position. She was told she could not move during this procedure, otherwise it could jeopardize the integrity of the pictures from the scan. Mommy nodded obediently as the technician spoke with her calmly yet firmly. They allowed me to pull a chair right next to my mother during the entire scan, which was greatly needed and even more appreciated than they could ever imagine.

The technician explained to Mom, "The machine will lower its top half down quite low over your body and take slow sweeps of your entire body in order to get pictures of every area that we have been directed to shoot. Once all of the film has been shot, you will have to wait a few minutes before getting off of the machine in order to ensure that all of what is needed is correct." He assured Mom that he and three others were in a booth where we could see them and there was a sound system into the room so that we could hear them or they us if necessary.

"Okay," mommy said timidly. I informed the technician that we were told we could bring music and handed him the CD and we were on our way.

As the door closed behind us, I scooted my chair close to Mom, took her hand, and said, "It's going to be fine, Mommy. This won't take that long."

The technician had put the worship music on for us, and turned on the speakers in the room where we were. The music sounded great, through a wonderful sound system, and with that, I could see my mother begin to be less tense and a bit more relaxed as I held her hand. Then we heard through the music and the speaker system, "We're going to begin now." As the machine began to lower over my mother's body I could see the look of hysteria coming over her face. She squeezed my hand so tightly that I wanted to scream, but I knew I couldn't, so I made a conscious effort to grin and bear it. I decided to start talking to her through my own squeals and anxiety over the crushing feeling on my hand.

"Mom, listen to the music. Come on, focus in on the music." I began to sing softly with the music to get her to think about the words. I wanted her to focus on whom and from where she could draw her strength. Her faith could surely take away any feelings of fear and anxiety. I sang and found comfort in it myself, which was a great help to both of us. As the machine passed her head down her body, I could feel her loosen her grip until it moved up toward her head. I began to pray with her in addition to listening to the music. Each time the grip tightened, we would send praises to the Lord. Soon the atmosphere began to change, and I could feel that Mom was no longer gripping my hand as tightly, but just enough to know I was there. All of what we were doing, singing and praying, could be heard at any time by the technicians in the booth behind us, which of course was fine with both Mom and me. Even at a time like this, if what they were witnessing could lead someone to ask about our relationship or a relationship with Christ for themselves, then to God be all the glory! We were doing the only things that we knew to do.

The entire procedure took about an hour and a half, which probably felt like three to my mother. But it was finally over and she was allowed to go into the changing waiting area. They wanted to make sure all of the pictures that were taken were as clear and precise as necessary. We waited in the changing area for about ten minutes and then were told we could leave. My mom breathed a sigh of relief and immediately proceeded to change into her clothing to go home. Mom was tired and although the day was not long, it was full, and because she had been so filled with anxiety at one point, she was mentally and physically drained. I remember asking what she wanted to do for dinner. There was a supermarket in the same area. It would have been simple to drive there and pick up something for dinner. My mother did not want to wait a minute longer; all she wanted to do was get back home and relax for the evening. Her desire was to pick up something quick with my stepfather and daughter in mind and to get home.

As we drove home, I began to tell mom how great she had done in this situation and I was thankful that it was over for her. We had been told that the MRI results would be sent to our oncologist, who would then contact us or we should contact them in about a week to set up an appointment. I assured my mother that I would be in contact within the appropriate amount of time if they did not contact us first. Her mind seemed to be at ease for now, but I knew part of it was due to her fatigue from the day. I had decided I would drop her off and call in pizza or something else that I would not have to cook since it was now so late in the day. I felt like I had worked the whole day, and I had. Going into the office first and then taking my mother to her MRI appointment did constitute a full day's work. Once I got her settled in, I checked on my daughter and asked her if she wanted to go with me to the store. "Yes Mommy!" she excitedly responded. She always desired and was willing to jump in the car and go anywhere with me. So off we traveled to pick up some take-out for dinner and to get home and prepare for the next day.

As usual, my morning started off with me getting Alex to the school bus and going back home to finish my preparation for work. Her school bus picked her up at 6:40 in the morning, which gave me plenty of time to get back home and ready for work.

After showering and dressing, I would go upstairs to my mother's house through the back stairs. We always left the back door open in case of an emergency, especially in the middle of the night if I needed to get to my mother. If she was still asleep, which, in many cases she was, I would go back downstairs and finish what I needed to do to get ready for work, go back upstairs and wake her to give her insulin and her medication prior to leaving for work. I would kiss her, tell her I loved her, and tell her to call me when she woke up. Of course, I realized she began to do less and less getting up on her own because the pain was so intense, so in my mind, I was preparing myself to go back on family leave until we got through this new crisis.

The doctor's office called within three days of the MRI appointment that we had been to, to schedule an appointment with our oncology doctor. Mom received the phone call and immediately called me at work to check my schedule. This was Wednesday and the appointment would be on the upcoming Monday in the morning, which gave me plenty of time to make the appropriate arrangements with my company. I had been there for almost five years and had not taken all of the accrued vacation since I was given three weeks per year. I spoke with my manager and we were all set for the appointment on the following Monday.

Monday arrived and I was a bit anxious this time. I had prayed all weekend about the appointment and knew God's sovereignty would always prevail, and I trusted Him. We drove to the doctor once again and the car was quiet. I turned on worship music because the quiet was just as uncomfortable as the feeling that we both had about this appointment, but neither of us would share it. We had arrived and gone through our normal routine of checking in and waiting to be called. As usual, the wait was not long at all, which in this case I'm not sure made us feel better or worse. We were taken into a room, but this time, there was no request for my mother's vital signs, and no need to undress. The doctor came in and greeted us, but I could tell his greeting was of a serious nature. He inquired about my mother's hip and how she felt overall. He proceeded to explain what the results of the MRI had shown them.

"Well, we now know why your mom has been in so much pain in her hip. It surprises me that she has been able to walk at all without screaming. Have you been able to sleep much?" he asked.

"Not really," she stated.

"Let me show you the film that we took from the MRI."

He put the film up on the display screen and guided us through what we saw. He showed us a picture of my mother's hip bone. There was a dark wide circle right on the hip, which he pointed to and said, "This is the cause of your mother's pain. The cancer has eaten a hole in her hip bone, which means it has spread to the bone area, and other areas of her body."

Oh my God! I thought. *It's back! No more remission, it is back!*

The doctor did not suggest radiation, or chemotherapy, but simply stated, "We can do those treatments again, but I think in this case it might make things worse rather than better. At this point, I don't think there is much else that we can do."

What?! I screamed in my head. *Nothing else you can do? Oh no, we are still in this fight! As long as my mother has breath, we are still in this fight! We have a relationship with the Master Physician, our Heavenly Father, the Lord, Jehovah Rophe, our healer. I knew if He said my mother would be healed, then she would.*

I would have faith until God said it was finished. I was still in shock, and could see my mom's eyes welling up with tears. The doctor said, "I'll give you a few moments and then we'll set up another appointment for about two weeks from now."

There was a box of Kleenex in the room, of which I handed a tissue to my mother and took one for myself. I could not stand to see her look so defeated, so defenseless, having been given this news. I had to pull myself together quickly in order to be there for her. I normally did all of my crying in private during my prayer time; she had never seen me cry while with her, especially during appointments. This time, it was different. We were told it was over before it was over, we were not accepting it, not until the one who had the final say said so.

The drive was entirely too quiet, with the exception of the sniffles that came from my mom. I kept saying, "Mommy, it's not over. We will continue to pray as we have been doing, and we know that God is with us." I just couldn't have her give up. The fight would be so much tougher if she gave up. "Please Mommy, don't give up. Stay with me. Hang in there."

My mother wanted nothing said to my stepfather, with the exception of the fact that the cancer had affected her hip bone. Once again, I felt that she was protecting him, and this time, I told her so. He needed to know what we knew, but unfortunately deep down, I think that she felt he had given up when he got the first report that she had cancer. Now the next step was to give my sister the shocking news from eleven hundred miles away. I knew I could not muster up the courage myself to tell her. I was truly depending on the Lord to deliver this message. I chose to call her soon after I got my mother settled in the house after the appointment. I was not going back to work and called my manager to tell her so. I simply stated I had received some news that was not so good at the appointment and that I would see her in the morning.

I called my sister and her reaction was just as I had expected, "What do you mean 'they're not going to do anything else'?"

"Just what I said, Shell. They think that any more treatment will cause more damage than good."

"So what do we do?"

"Pray" I said, "just pray. We have an actual appointment with the doctor in two weeks, and I'll know more at that point. I think he did not want to hit us with so much today." I could tell how hard this news was for her to take at all, much less by telephone and with such distance between us. I could hear her sniffles over the phone as I did the same thing while dealing with the pain that we both had, for our mother, and for each other.

Two weeks had gone by quickly and it was time for the appointment. While at work, I had discussed with my boss the probability of having to go back on family leave full-time in order to care for my mother. She suggested I contact the Human Resource department to get the appropriate paperwork to reactivate my family leave in order to take it to the appointment with me. I did everything necessary and had the paperwork with me on the day of the appointment. This time, my mother said nothing on the way to the appointment. We prayed, but she moaned when getting into the car and moaned when getting out. She slept even less now and I could see her condition deteriorating.

We checked in and waited to be called. The nurse called us and we went to the room. Mom undressed and we waited for the doctor to arrive. There was a knock at the door and we both said "come in" at the same time. There was her doctor, who had been so wonderful to us, looking a bit sad, yet realizing we were still fighting. He took all of her vital signs, and her blood sugar levels, and said it would be fine to continue the insulin for now. He prescribed some pain medication for her hip and gave us the name of a person in the department that handles specialty patient care. It was not time to get a hospital bed put into my mother's room yet, but it was coming and the doctor wanted us be prepared and ahead of the game. He also gave me hospice information and the Visiting Nurse Association contact since Mom would need a visiting nurse eventually.

This was all too overwhelming for me. We had reached a new level of her illness, and one that we had to prepare for with such finality.

"How is your hip was feeling?"

"It hurts pretty badly, doctor."

"I suggest that you walk and move as little as possible." Whatever she felt most comfortable doing do it. "Ms. Paige, are you going to be with her full-time or is there someone that can stay with her full-time from this point on?" "It is going to be increasingly difficult for her to get around by herself, and we do not want her to fall and break any bones or do any additional damage."

"I will be with her full-time. In fact, I have a form that needs to be filled out before I leave your office today." He took the form and said he would fill it out while I helped her get dressed. The doctor said her vitals were great, and he would see us again in about three weeks and left the room. After a few moments, he came back into the room and handed me the completed form. As I glanced at it, it stated my mother had lung cancer and that it had metastasized or spread to other parts of her body that were listed on the paper. I shrieked inside when reading it. I had never seen anything on paper stating this information.

I called him back in and said, "Can I see you for a second in the hall?" He stepped out and I said, "You never told me that my mother had cancer in all of these areas—liver, pancreas, lungs, brain, bone." Although I of course knew about the lungs and brain and now bone, but now he had added two new areas to the list. I felt like dropping to my knees right there in front of the doctor. The feeling of defeat started to overwhelm me, but I could not let it. For I was the one who said and believed it is not finished until God says it is finished!

The doctor responded, "I'm sorry, but this is where we are with the cancer at this point. She has about three months to live."

My body went totally numb, I could barely utter more than "thank you."

He said, "I'm really sorry. Your mother is a wonderful woman." I stood still for a moment in silence, knowing what this man had just said, but not believing he said it to me. Three months! Three months! How can anyone put a time limit on someone else's life? These were my thoughts as the doctor walked away in silence. I turned around, turned the knob on the door behind me, changed my composure completely, and smiled to my mother and said, "Are you ready to get home?"

Her answer was expected. "Yes, I am tired, in pain, and I need to lie down."

Upon arriving home, I called my office and told my manager that I would not be back that day. I explained in less detail what had happened at the appointment and said I would bring the paper-work to Human Resources. This time, there was no discussion of working from home. Working from this point on would mean caring for my mother. This was one time that I did not want to call my sister with an update. I didn't know how to tell her what the doctor had just told me. So, I waited until finally, one evening a few days later, I got up the courage to call her. She was speechless. There was a stream of silence between us over the phone as I explained I had said nothing to Mommy and had no plans to tell her. We both decided to let her go to digest what she'd just been told. The plan was that she would call me to let me know how soon she would be able to make the trip back to Boston.

It had been two weeks since we were at our last appointment and I had contacted a patient liaison about getting my mother a hospital bed. We had determined she could no longer sleep in her regular bed. The pain had become too intense and she was too weak to pull herself up on her own. A hospital bed would help with some of these issues. The liaison also suggested that we get my mom a visiting nurse that would come in daily to check her vital signs and do the necessary blood work on her. After making the necessary phone calls to schedule what was needed, within three to four days, all of these things were put into place, and the nurse would be coming to meet us at the end of the week.

By the beginning of the following week, my mother's bedroom had been turned into a home hospital room. The hospital bed had been delivered and set up. An intravenous pump had also been delivered that would administer fluids and any necessary medications into my mother's veins. The Visiting Nurses Association had scheduled a nurse that came in to teach me how to work with the equipment. I was taught how to change the fluid bags and to operate the settings on the machine when necessary. Only the nurses could create the lines into her veins, which was fine with me. Finally, we would meet our regular visiting nurse. We were blessed with a wonderful visiting nurse by the name of Ed. He had a great personality and had been working with terminally ill patients for a long time. He found himself in a different setting with us, as he mentioned on a few occasions. First, we were a family whose members were Christians, believing in the power of God, the power of prayer, and we had great faith. Secondly, he could see my mother for the strength that she still had, even through the pain and weakness that the cancer now caused her. I looked forward to Ed's arrival each morning as he looked forward to seeing me at the door. Ed's schedule was to come in every weekday morning around 9:30 to check my mother's vital signs. He was as cheery as I was and we continued to cheer each other on during the course of his visits. In addition, for me, he was a welcomed relief, especially if Mom had a difficult night and I was up during most of it with her.

My sister had flown in over the weekend and this morning would be her first time meeting Ed and I looked forward to making that introduction. She had heard so much about everything going on and my interactions with everyone involved with our family, but it was a much greater feeling for us both when she could put names with faces. The doorbell rang and I had not quite made it upstairs yet; I had just finished some quiet time in prayer. Most days, I was already upstairs with my mother, but if I did not make it downstairs from my mother's house, Ed knew to ring the doorbell of my home and I would answer, run upstairs, and then down my mother's front stairs to let him in. This morning, my sister awaited Ed's arrival with anticipation. We had put an extra mattress and box spring on the floor of the dining room to accommodate my sister during her stay. There was no more sleeping space in my mother's house. She was in the hospital bed and my stepfather was in the guest room, which left no space for a guest. The sleeping arrangement was not at all uncomfortable with the exception of its location. But we were family and we had no problem with anything at this point. Our focus was on mom's comfort, not our own.

Mom was still in great spirits despite her pain and discomfort. She adored Ed and he adored her. My sister had immediately taken a liking to Ed and felt extremely comfortable with him. He had now become part of the family. My daughter didn't see him because she was gone to school by the time he arrived in the mornings and he only stayed an hour or so at most, but she heard much about him. Mom was still able to get in and out of the bed with assistance so I would make sure she was washed and dressed before Ed's arrival as my sister did on this particular morning. It was wonderful how Shellie could fill in when she came home and begin as though she was never so far away. I appreciated that about her; she was eager to learn and to help. I would show her and she would be on her way, doing what needed to be done. She had, over the weekend already, learned how to change the fluid bags on the machine that my mother was hooked up to and how to clear the line if there was a clog. If my mom had to go to the bathroom which was now less and less because she ate less and less, Shellie had learned how to maneuver my mother in and out of the bathroom with the machine or to disconnect my mother temporarily.

I blessed God for feeling so secure in her being willing and capable of helping, which unfortunately was not the same feeling that I had with my step-father. As much as I tried to understand my step-father's difficulty with accepting and coping with the situation as it was, I could not help but feel a degree of anger and resentment toward him for his actions during my mother's illness. Although I had never been married, I did not imagine that during a time like this, a spouse and mate would be so distant. I believed the person that you had pledged "till death do you part" with would be at your side until you took your last breath. It was painful to watch his lack of interaction with my mother or her condition. He was so disconnected that I had to force him to lend any assistance whatsoever when it was necessary. He was now retired from the full-time job that he had held for over twenty years. He had a part-time job at a local restaurant which was within walking distance from home, where he worked until around noon each day. He would walk through my mother's bedroom to get to the kitchen or the den from the top of the stairs after entering the front door, greet us or her, and proceed to watch television or nap for the rest of the day. I would be up and downstairs between my house and Mom's, and not once did I come back up and interrupt a visit with my mother from him, or a meal that he tried to feed her, or any interaction at all. If my mother wanted something, she would simply pick up the telephone and call me, and if I asked where my stepfather was, my mother would state he had gone out for a while or napping in the den and he probably did not hear her. I found myself constantly asking the Lord to help me not to stay so angry with him, because I did not want it to grow into disrespect.

In addition, I could feel my desire for marriage and a mate changing. Not that I no longer had the desire, but I did not want the enemy to make me fear that my mate would treat me in the same way if I were to ever get sick. I began to realize I was hurt and disappointed by what I experienced and saw through my stepfather. I knew there was more to his undesirable actions during my mother's illness as I began to piece his whereabouts and habits together, but the worst of it was that my mother found out as well.

I received a phone call one afternoon from my mother to come upstairs immediately. She was on the side of the hospital bed and said she had just received a phone call. The woman on the other end of the phone asked for my stepfather. The person said she knew of my mother's illness but was told she was his sister. She proceeded to volunteer information that Mom found extremely difficult to handle. Needless to say, she was crushed. I could see the look of pain and despair on her face. All I remember thinking through my anger, pain, and disappointment was how could this man who claimed he loved my mother, be married to her for ten years, and do this while she was on her death bed? I would never have begrudged him meeting someone else after her death and living a happy remarried life, but now? All I could do is look at my mom through her tears and tell her how sorry I was. I tried to help her find comfort in understanding that everyone deals with pain differently and maybe he knew no other way to deal with his pain. My problem was that I had to convince myself as well without her knowing.

I wondered if my mom was ever the same after that day. My sister was back in Alabama and I remember calling her and telling her what happened, and of course she was in shock and angry. For both my sister and me, our pain was that my mother had to find out at this point in her illness. We consoled each other and talked more about Mom's medical status. We could do nothing about what had happened, but only prepare to deal with what would lie ahead.

My mother's condition had worsened. She was now at a point where she was unable to get up out of the bed and would need adult diapers. I was so concerned with caring for her. I wanted to give her the best care that I could. I wanted her to be clean and not feel any more discomfort than she already felt. Her pain was now excruciating and Ed, our visiting nurse, had requested that the doctor prescribe Morphine since the Oxycontin and the Oxycodone that she had been taking over the past year were no longer effective. He had also suggested I plan for someone from hospice to come in and visit with us in order to transfer my mother into hospice care if necessary. I knew my mom's wishes were to stay at home, so as much as the hospice representatives and I discussed the possibilities, we all knew my mother would not be going into a hospice facility. I still maintained that the Lord could heal her at any point, and it was not over until my mother took her last breath.

My sister was about to make another trip home to see our mom and she knew I was growing weary, especially after all that had transpired with my stepfather the month before. She knew this trip was a necessary one, and she wanted to see mommy as many times as possible at this point in her illness. I eagerly awaited her arrival for about a week or so. Somehow I knew I had to make some additional decisions regarding her trip home and then back to Alabama. I had decided to send my daughter, then eleven, back with my sister. I felt as though my mother, her Nauni, was to a point in her illness that I did not want my daughter to see and carry in her memories of my mother. I had prayed about this and knew it was the right decision. The difficult part was we had never been apart, other than a sleepover here and there with my dad and stepmom. Other than those times, it was not a practice for me to allow her to sleepover at other people's homes. This was a big one for me. It was also an additional responsibility for my sister, although temporary. It was still summer-time and Alex could enjoy the rest of the summer with her cousin Noah and come back home before school began. I knew the one thing that I had not thought about through all of this decision making was that I would send my daughter away in preparation for the passing of my mother. As much as I knew the God that I served was sovereign and could heal her in an instant, there was that inevitable thought and reality that it might not be on this earth, but in His loving arms in Heaven.

Finally, the day had arrived when I would drive to the airport to pick up my sister. It was a hot summer day, and my mother was glad that my sister was coming again. Although she was in the bed most of the time at this point, she could sit up for a while, but she was extremely weak. Shellie arrived and I can remember this day so vividly, because on the way from the airport, I told my sister that I had to stop at the pharmacy to pick up another medication for Mom. I don't quite remember what the medication was, but the experience forever stays in my mind. My sister and I were at the pharmacy, which was in the same building where the HMO was that our family belonged to. There was an extremely long hallway from one entrance to the other of the building, and the elevators would also take you to the doctor's offices. In this case, we only needed to stay in the pharmacy area, because her prescription had been called in. I went into the line as my sister took a seat that was a bit of a distance from where the line was. I finally got to the front of the line and was told that I would have to wait a few minutes for the prescription. I sat with my sister to wait to be called.

When I was finally called, my sister came up with me. There was an elderly woman at the other end of the counter picking up a prescription as well. The pharmacy technician told her the price of the prescription, which I remember being well over $300 and her insurance, for whatever reason, would not cover the cost. She explained to him that she did not have enough money to purchase such an expensive prescription and he shook his head and plainly stated he did not know what to tell her. The look of fright, then pain, and finally, the tears that began to flow from this woman's face was the most heart wrenching scene I thought I would ever see. My sister and I had to sit down before leaving to compose ourselves for a moment. We were going through so much pain and grief at the time, but to witness this woman's pain hurt far more on this day than the reality that we were living. She and I both sat and cried. Neither of us were able to assist this woman financially with her need, otherwise we both commented that we would whip out a checkbook in a heartbeat if we could, to pay for her prescription, and then to deal with the emotional toll that our own situation was taking on us was more than we could bear, at that moment.

As we sat, we talked about the fact that our mother was dying, and the reality of it was too much at times. We talked about how much this did not seem to be reality, but it was indeed ours. As we cried there together in that long hallway that echoed with every sniffle, we tried to compose ourselves enough to leave that place and head to the house and enter it, looking like we were fine for Mommy's sake. Our mother had yet to discuss any type of final affairs with us, because I know that she was not ready to leave us, or to even discuss the possibility. I had hinted a few times prior, but she never wanted to go into full discussion, so I left it alone. I knew enough about my mother's affairs and since between my sister and me, I was living in the state, she knew that I could handle whatever needed to be handled. Mom did have a will that outlined her wishes clearly so there would be no mistakes. I did not want to discuss these matters either, even though I knew it would be inevitable. At one point I remember thinking I would have loved for Mom to do what I had seen in a few movies from people that were dying. I wanted her to make some videotapes for her grandchildren. Noah was only five and lived out of state and there was my daughter. I wanted her to leave them something to watch and listen to, but again, I think that it was just too difficult for her to come to grips with.

My sister and I traveled up the front stairs of my mother's house directly into her bedroom, where my mom lit up when she saw Shellie. This time, the difficulty for Shellie was not in what she didn't expect a year ago, but more because of what she *did* expect. Mom was fighting for her life, and now the battle seemed to be closing in.

Shellie stayed for about four days, and pitched in as usual. She now had the routines down and I could sleep in a little later. I remember during one of the conversations that I had with her. I realized I was just emotionally and physically beat down.

I had a support system of a small group of friends, and my mother's best friend whom she called her sister. Evelyn had no sisters and my mother was an only child. They had struck up a friendship back when my mother was first saved and they attended the same church. Evelyn would come and take over for me on Sundays every once and a while so that I could attend church. She loved my mother so much, like a little sister, and would never let Mom forget it. Her family and children loved Mom as much as she did, and the two families blended quite well. Evelyn made sure we knew she was only a phone call away. She had proven it on a few occasions by jumping in her car and driving the forty-minute ride into Boston from her house within a moment's notice to check on Mom, or bring something that was needed. Evelyn wanted to see Shellie while she was here this time, so she made sure she was around to spend time with us.

As soon as Shellie walked in, she put down her bag and got on the hospital bed with Mom. She held Mommy and talked with her, and I loved to see that; it was something special between the two of them. For me, the special moments between Mom and I would be when she would ask me to sit next to her hospital bed, and pray with and read the Bible to her, I appreciated that time with her.

A few days had gone by since my sister's arrival and we had lots of company in and out of the house.

From church members to some of my friends, it seemed to be a bit of a busy time, at least for the first few days of my sister's arrival. Ed, our visiting nurse, was there every day at this point to brighten up my mother's and our day as we brightened up his. Mom tended to sleep more at this point, which was unusual to us, but nevertheless, she was at a different stage of her illness.

It was a Saturday night, my sister's last night there, and she would be leaving with my daughter in the morning. I had made the arrangements through the airline to have them move my sister's seating around in order for my daughter to travel with her. My little one merely thought that she was going to enjoy the rest of her summer vacation with her auntie, uncle, and cousin in Birmingham before school started. She knew she would miss me, but she also knew she would only be going for a few weeks and then she'd be back home.

Sunday morning had finally arrived and the time always felt too short to me. But I had my daughter all packed and ready to go, and I was going to take Shellie and her to the airport. We all went into mom's room to say good morning and spend a little time before they left for the airport.

Something was different about my mother on that particular morning. She had difficulty speaking. Her speech was slurred and unclear and not only that, she was dipping in and out of sleep.

My sister kept saying to her, "Mommy, can you hear me? Do you understand what I am saying?"

There was of course not much time for my sister to stay with me to figure out what was going on, so she had to leave. I can only imagine how difficult it was for her to leave our mom in that state, not knowing what was going on and not being able to stay to find out in person. She knew she would eventually find out by phone, but it was not the same.

My daughter asked on several occasions as they left, "What's the matter with Nauni, Mommy? Why is she talking like that?"

I simply stated "Nauni is not feeling well today, so she is having a hard time talking." Little did we realize at the time that our mom, at that point, had begun to slip into a coma. I took the girls to the airport as worried as they were and promised to call them with any updates as soon as I got them. As I made them promise to call as soon as they arrived in Birmingham. We kissed and hugged and said our goodbyes and my sister promised again to call when she arrived in Birmingham, especially this time because she had my daughter with her.

I arrived back home from the airport and felt the emptiness of my house before I had entered it. My daughter had left me for the first time in her life. My eyes welled up with tears and I am not sure whether it was more because I already missed her or because I needed strength to handle what I was about to be faced with alone. As I got out of the car, I braced myself for where this particular road with my mom would take us. When I was at the top of the stairs to her house and entered her bedroom, she was awake but not talking. Somehow, I think she knew she was slipping and it was frustrating to her because she could not control it. I put a call into the after-hours number that we were given in order for them to page our nurse Ed and waited for a return phone call as I sat at my mother's bedside.

Ed returned my phone call and asked what I was seeing and hearing. Although I was not a medical professional, Ed knew how capable I was at caring for my mother and could tell what was going on from my descriptions and observations of her over the last twenty-four hours. He gave a preliminary confirmation of my observation. He gave instruction that if anything were to begin to happen, like a fever or what looked to be a seizure, to call 911 and have her taken to the hospital. There was not much else for me to do at this point. Mom had stopped eating a few weeks before and now all that was left was to keep her clean, and make sure her sheets were changed. When my sister called that evening, I gave her the news and assured her that I would call her once Ed came to the house. I slept upstairs on the mattress and box spring on the floor in the dining room outside of my mother's bedroom so that I could be close and hear her if she needed me.

Upon Ed's arrival the next morning, he checked all of my mom's vital signs and confirmed what we had discussed the night before. He explained further that she would lose control of her bladder and that I should probably invest in some adult diapers. He was not concerned about bowel movements because she had stopped taking in food. He also got the doctor to prescribe some morphine that he knew I would have to give my mother because she was losing control of her own muscular abilities and the pain would worsen as time went on. There would be no hospice care because home was where Mommy wanted to be and home was where she would stay. Although I was being told to prepare for the end, I still believed God could heal her and it was not over until she took her last breath.

I went out that day and followed Ed's instructions. I frantically ordered several boxes of adult diapers, enough to open a store, and picked up the prescription for the morphine. I got home with the diapers and put a few boxes of them in the garage not thinking that her time was drawing down and she really didn't need so many boxes. Since it was summer I was not concerned about having to go out into the cold if I ran out of the supply in the house. I had not yet had to use the diapers, which was a bit of a relief but I knew I would need them eventually. I began giving her morphine under her tongue for the pain as soon as I brought it home from the pharmacy.

The nurse said it would be fine to begin administering as soon as I got it. The doses were small and I could tell that as she needed it, it would bring relief. She had not completely slipped into the coma so we had developed our own way of communicating over a period of a few days.

On one particular morning I woke up, checked on my mom, and her sheets were soaked. I remember thinking, *okay, it is done the way I see them do it in the hospital so I can do this, just roll her over on each side of her body.* The only problem was that I was alone and my mother was in excruciating pain. She had soaked everything—sheets and nightgown. I knew I would not be able to move her too often so I figured once I got her diaper on, she at least would not soak the sheets daily. I stood at her bedside and lowered the rail down on the hospital bed. I did not let it down all of the way, because I needed to protect her from rolling onto the floor as I attempted to roll her over onto one side. When I tried to initially move her by pushing on her hip to roll her over, she swung at me. I could see the look of intense pain on her face.

"Oh Mommy, I am sorry. I don't mean to hurt you, I just want to get you dry." I tried again, and she swung again. At this point, I realized this was not as easy as changing a baby's diaper. I opened up this adult diaper and because I was unable to move her I had no way to get it on her. There she lay, in these sheets and nightgown that were soaked, and I refused to leave my mother in that condition. I tried to move her and began to plead with her, saying, "Mommy, please help me. I can't do this alone. I want to get you dry."

As I said it, I stood at my mother's bedside, every emotion that had been suppressed, now surfacing. I was broken and crying because what had appeared to be in my mind, such a simple task, keeping her clean and comfortable, now felt impossible. At that moment, my stepfather walked up the stairs, took one look into the room at my attempts to accomplish this feat, walked past me, mumbled hello and went into his room, closed the door, and never returned. I stood there, astonished and sobbing. All I wanted now, was to make sure that my mom, whom I loved so deeply, was comfortable. Was that too much to ask?

"Oh, my God! Please help me, please help me. I just want her comfortable, Lord. I just want to keep her clean." I could not allow my mother to lay like this and what would I do from now on? What was going to happen? As I sobbed at my mother's bedside and pleaded with her to allow me to move her, the doorbell rang. I had been so wrapped up with this situation that I had no idea what time it was. I went downstairs and it was Ed. The Lord, in His grace and mercy, had sent Ed at the perfect time. I opened the door and he took one look at my swollen, tearstained face and said, "What's wrong?"

I could barely get the words out between sobs. "I can't do . . . I just want her clean . . . I can't do it, she won't let me."

He physically turned me around and headed me up the stairs to see what I was talking about. He looked at me with sorrowful eyes and said, "I'm sorry."

Although this was not his responsibility to ask, he asked, "Where is your stepfather?" I told him and he physically guided me into the kitchen, sat me down in a chair, and said, "You stay here and relax. Your stepfather and I will handle this."

He knocked on my stepfather's door and told him that he wanted his help and my stepfather exited the room and followed Ed to my mother's bedside. I remember sitting at that kitchen table, numb and weak, tired and worn. I had been through so much over the past year and a half, a pillar of strength. This one episode left me like a Raggedy Ann doll. It felt like all of the strength that I had through every other situation during my mother's illness could not bear me up this time. Once Ed and my stepfather had completed the task of getting my mother changed and cleaned up, he came in the kitchen to check on me.

"Are you okay?" he asked.

I looked up at him as he seemed to tower over me at six feet and me at five feet-two and now sitting in a chair. "Yes, I am better now." I thanked him and came back into the room with him to see that my mother was fine, and fresh and clean, which Ed knew would please me. During the months that he had spent with us every day, he knew how important Mom's complete care was to me, and commented on it on several occasions. During our conversation on this particular morning, Ed told me that he did not know how much time, but based on his experience and expertise with terminally ill patients, my mother did not have long until she passed. There were some concerns that he warned me about with lung cancer patients that were a bit gory, but I listened and took instructions as he gave them.

Another two days had passed and I knew that my mother was slipping away. She could not speak, and I was not sure that she could hear me any longer, but something in my heart told me that she could. This particular morning, I called my sister and told her to get on a plane. I knew Mom would wait for her but she needed to come now. I went to my mother's bedside and told her, "Shellie's coming Mommy, just hold on. I know you want her here, so she is coming."

My sister arrived that evening and I picked her up at the airport. She had left my daughter back in Birmingham with my brother-in-law and nephew while she came to be at my mother's bedside with me until the end. When she arrived to the house, she rushed upstairs to make sure Mom had not gone on yet.

With relief, she stood at our mother's bed-side, with her eyes welling up with tears she said, "Mommy, I'm here. I'm here, Mommy. It's Shellie."

We both told her how much we loved her and that it was okay to go now. We would be okay; she had fought a good fight, but it was now time to rest. Even though we had no immediate proof, we believed she heard us. She laid now in a deep coma, where her breathing was loud and rattled as though it was difficult to breathe.

That night, Shellie and I moved a mattress onto the floor of my mother's bedroom so that we could sleep in the room beside her bed. At approximately

4:30 that morning, my mother let out a loud gasp and took her last breath.

My sister rolled over and tapped me and asked, "Did you hear that?"

"Yeah," I replied. Neither of us moved for a moment.

Then my sister got up and went to my mother's bedside and said, "She's gone."

There was no wailing, no screaming and crying from my sister or me. God had given us a peace; in fact, He had given all of us—I believe my mother included—a peace. We knew where she was going, so we were relieved to see her pain and suffering gone. Our mom was gone, the one who walked around in her body was gone and that brought sadness, but the relief of no more pain and suffering for her was so much greater that we could bare the loss.

Oddly enough, at the time of my mother's death, we were unable to call anyone because of the hour, so Shellie and I sat on the mattress in that same room where we slept that night with our mother at our side and reminisced about all the beautiful times that we had spent with Mom as children through adulthood. We did go to my stepfather's room to inform him of my mother's passing and left the bedroom where my mother was in order to allow him some time to spend with her. By this time, it was daylight and we had called Ed, who called the hospital and made all of the necessary arrangements to have mom removed from home.

When Ed arrived, he made sure that he was at the house before the coroner. He told my sister and me to stay in the kitchen as the coroner arrived. My stepfather had left the house by this time to grieve in his own way. Ed came into the kitchen to have me sign the death certificate, gave my sister and me his condolences and a hug, and we watched them drive away.

My sister and I quietly walked back up the stairs, through my mother's room, knowing she had fought this fight until the end.

Chapter 12

THERE'S NO PLACE LIKE HOME

As my sister and I arrived at the airport to pick up my daughter, nephew, and brother-in-law, I still wondered how I would tell my daughter about her Nauni. Noah was five so he would not comprehend the magnitude of what had happened like my daughter would. In addition, Alex had been brought up here in Boston with her Nauni and saw her daily. I had asked my brother-in-law not to say anything to Alex about my mother's passing. I wanted to be the one to break the news once she had arrived home.

Shellie and I were parked at the arrival gate, and saw them coming through the doors. My daughter ran toward me, as I stood with a half-smile on my face, grieving my mother and overjoyed to see my daughter.

"Mommy!" she yelled as she ran into my arms through the door.

"Hi sweetie, how are you?"

"I'm fine Mommy. I missed you."

"I missed you too, baby. I am so glad you're back home."

Then the question came. "How's Nauni?" I did not respond and acted as though I did not hear her, as I put her bag in the car. My sister and brother-in-law remained silent.

"Mommy, did you hear me? How is Nauni?"

"Mommy needs to tell you about Nauni, sweetie."

"Why? What's wrong, Mommy?"

"Nauni died while you were away, sweetie."

The color immediately left her face and she bent over as though she was going to collapse. She began to sob uncontrollably and we had to carry her to the car sobbing in my arms. She asked in between sobs when Nauni had died and why I didn't tell her. My only response was that I did not feel that she could handle it. She was quiet, laying against the window in the backseat of the car. Noah didn't understand what he had seen, but asked why Alex was crying. His mom told him that Alex had just received some bad news and it made her sad. He tried his best at five to console his cousin and it appeared to make her feel a bit better.

As we arrived at the house, my daughter found it difficult to go upstairs to my mother's house initially. We had already begun to receive calls about the arrangements for my mother's funeral service. My sister and I had scheduled an appointment

with a nearby funeral home that had a fine reputation throughout the community. We were still
in the midst of making phone calls to family and
friends to let them know of my mother's passing.
The church where we were members was wonderful. My mother was the head of the missionary
department and was loved by the ministry. Our
fellow church members brought over food daily;
we never had to cook a meal from the time that my
mother passed until after the funeral.

We had several family meetings between my
sister, brother-in-law, a few close pastors including
our pastor who would be officiating, and some close
friends to assist us in making plans for the service.
Since my mother was the head of a ministry at
our church and within the church organization,
there would be official activities that would be done
during the service. She had also gone through a
Ministers-in-Training course held at our church a
few years prior with me and we graduated together.
The official part of the service would be a processional of all of the ordained ministers, deacons,
elders, the presiding bishop, and pastor of our
church. It seemed like a big to-do, especially since
Mom was not one for that type of fanfare. However,
I am sure that she would have been quite honored
by such a processional marking her service and
love for our church.

As my sister and I began the grueling plans
for my mother's home-going service, we had to
schedule a date for the actual service. We had to
keep in mind those traveling from out-of-state,
which made it a bit difficult because we didn't want

to prolong our grief any longer than necessary. However, out of fairness to others we were going to wait a full week before having the service. Two days had now passed since my mother's death and we had begun to receive beautiful plants and flowers in sympathy for our loss. The house became so filled that instead of what would have been thought to bring a level of comfort, became a depressing reminder that we all only get one mother in a lifetime and she departed early from us.

There was so much to do. Mom had always spoken out about how she wanted to be buried when her time came. She had a will, which was no problem, but there was no need to consult that document to know and remember how strongly she felt about her service. She had chosen to be cremated. Her one adamant desire was not to have her children, friends, and family standing over a gravesite where she had just been buried, but to be cremated. As my sister and I both knew this was her wish from many years past, and remained the same throughout the years up until her death, there was no need to look for confirmation from any other source. We would do as our mom had asked. Since my mother had given her life to Christ, we knew where her spirit was going, and her body was just that: a body that would be turned to dust faster than if it were buried. My sister and I had no plans for keeping the remains in an urn or anything of that nature. We were merely doing what she had asked. Now it was time to go to the funeral home and go forth with making the actual plans for Mom's remains.

It was absolutely amazing to me, to witness what happens in the midst of planning a loved one's funeral service and the actual business of the funeral. My sister and I went through many emotions during the time that we spent with the funeral director's assistant. Initially, when we arrived, the funeral director was with another family so the assistant was kind enough to begin the process with us. The first thing was sympathy for us during our time of loss, accompanied by how much they knew we loved our mother, and then finally the book. We were then handed the book with the casket choices, no prices printed, but of course if we asked about a particular casket, we were then given the price. My sister and I began to realize how much of a business funerals were. Of course, the staff was not without sympathy and compassion, however, we could see how the sympathy for a family could be used as a sales tool during this great time of grief. We were given prices from $5,000 to $25,000, depending upon how much we loved our dear beloved departed. We looked at one another and realized Mom would have turned in her grave had we even considered spending $25,000 to burn a casket that she would only be in for about ten minutes. We decided upon one at a much lower cost than $25,000, especially because its only use would be for cremating.

Finally, the funeral director came in, introduced herself, and you could see she was filled with compassion but tired. She was tall in stature, but worn—I would guess merely by the nature of her business. My sister and I immediately felt a sense of compassion for this woman, much greater than our own loss, at least for that moment. We had decided upon a casket and confirmed it with the funeral director, along with the date which we would confirm with our pastor. We had confirmed our mom would be cremated, however there would be no service for this portion of her funeral. Only we, her family, would be part of the cremating service. All that would be made public was that there would be no interment after the homegoing service.

My sister and I had decided to make our mother's service what we perceived to be a real "homegoing" service and that once we sent her home at this service, it would indeed be finished. A new day had dawned in our lives after our experience at the funeral home on the day before. We wanted to celebrate our mother's life, and felt this was what she would have wanted. Her joy once she had given her life to Christ was infectious and we wanted her to be remembered in that way. We wanted people not to cry, but to rejoice with us for the life of our mother. We even wanted them to remember her homegoing service in the way that they remembered her. Not with sadness, but with joy, and we were determined to make that happen. We decided it might be difficult for people to see Mom laying at the front of the church, as there were those that were truly affected by her presence of life and even her battle for it while she was ill. She remained healthy looking throughout her illness, not eaten up by the disease so that people had a difficult time at times remembering she was sick until she could no longer function and come to the church services. Even through her weight loss, which is common in cancer patients, the loss was not devastating to her body, but complimentary, and she wore it well. I would say her appearance remained beautiful, as would most everyone, only by the glory of God until we closed the casket for the final time.

My sister and I got to work on how we would send our mom home. Always keeping in mind that we were not sad—we missed her, but we knew where she was and that brought joy to our hearts. We did not want to have any black at the funeral, so we told our pastor that our preference was everything and everyone in white, from the choir to the processional—even the ushers were to wear white. We gave our pastor a list of songs for the choir to sing that were all upbeat; no sad songs, no funeral hymns. We wanted foot-tapping, hand-clapping music—the music that mom sang to and loved! We informed the funeral home that we were to have white limousines and a white limousine carry her casket. The family would all wear white, even down to the littlest ones, her grandchildren. We did not desire lots of funeral bouquets so we asked that donations be made to the American Cancer Society in her name. We even dressed Mom in a favorite beautiful white suit. As a funeral program, we chose to put together a book of pictures of her and called it "Stages of Life" and showed the many stages of her life, some poetry, and a few descriptions. How amazing it was to see the finished product. My sister and I began to fill with excitement as we realized that we were truly sending mommy home the way she would have wanted to go; it would have excited her to see this all taking shape. Finally, what we considered to be the crescendo to this service: we ordered over two hundred white balloons to send off at the end of the homegoing service as a tribute to Mom's life.

The day had arrived. All of the planning that we had been doing for Mom's homegoing service would have led an onlooker to believe we had planned a fiftieth anniversary or birthday party, not a funeral. Yet, indeed it was a funeral, and all of our planning for this momentous occasion had taken our grief and turned it into joy. We could no longer look at this day as an impending day of doom and gloom, but a real party that we were about to host. As hard as it might have been for anyone else to believe, a sense of excitement rang in the air. No, we were not crazy; we loved Mom so much that we wanted to be whole for her, not broken down and we had the Lord as our strength! We could do this with God's help, and we were going to make it through this! In addition, I had personally realized many people were and had been watching me throughout this whole ordeal from the beginning of my mother's illness until the end. My trust in the Lord, my faith in Him through this walk in a barren land, would be a testimony for years to come. I might never have to give a word, but live in and through this experience, and the Lord would do the rest.

As our white limousine pulled up to the church, the white funeral hearse was in front and there were cars parked up and down on both sides of the streets and some of the adjacent streets. There was a lump in my throat. We were dressed in all of this beautiful white, going to say goodbye to Mom for the last time, on this earth, that is. As we filed out of the limo, it was a nice August evening, not too hot—in fact, it was just right for New England weather. The service was at 6:00 so that the heat of the day had already faded.

We began to make the journey up the church steps and were met at the front door by the church ushers, all of which I knew because I was a member of that usher board. I continued to serve with them when assigned until I could no longer attend services due to my mother's critical condition.

As we entered, the head usher smiled, gave me a hug, and nodded for us to enter. We entered the foyer of the church and waited for the processional, which was just arriving down the stairs to enter the sanctuary. There was a long processional of ministers, elders, and deacons led by our pastor, who was also the presiding bishop. All of this looked so formal, it almost made me want to salute! The choir was in the choir stand singing the wonderful songs that my mother loved and led by one of her favorite singers in the choir. She had nicknamed my mother "Mama Deloatch" and my mother loved responding to that term of endearment. There was motion for the family to now enter the sanctuary.

As we entered the sanctuary, the white that we had chosen to wear stood out beautifully. We looked throughout the sanctuary and every seat was filled, including the balcony areas. This was a standing room only event! So many had come to pay their respects to her and had no idea that they were in for the party of a lifetime. As we moved into our seats, I could feel how God had graced our family with the strength that we needed to live through these moments with joy, even down to the littlest grandchild.

As I looked in front of us at my mother's casket, it was set up as we had requested. Closed for those who could not face seeing her, although she looked beautiful, fully made up in all of her white. We had seen to it that the funeral home used her favorite makeup, and lipstick, she needed to look like herself, and she did. We decided to put a few of the pictures that were in the funeral program that we had framed on her casket during the service. My sister and I had prepared our own individual pieces to say during the service and I asked my daughter to prepare something to say to everyone about her Nauni. My stepfather had chosen not to say anything during the service as he felt he would not be able to remain calm enough.

The singing and clapping to the songs that were upbeat and perfect for the occasion left every eye dry. This was our goal: people smiled and clapped and sang and stood-up and praised the Lord! As I scanned the sanctuary, I could see some in amazement as to what they saw and experienced. They were having fun, at a funeral!

My pastor had a few words to say, and then he began to call up the members of the family to say what they wanted to say. Because Noah was only five, they started with the next grandchild, my daughter, and she bravely took the stairs up into the pulpit by herself and talked about her Nauni. I was amazed, proud, and grateful to the Lord for giving her the strength and fortitude to do this on her own without breaking. She came down from the pulpit and stepped down the stairs with such grace I could hardly contain myself. Next was my sister, whose strength and courage I so admired. This had been such a hard road for her being so far away. She did not get the full spectrum of experience in this illness. Each aspect of it seemed to be thrust upon her whether she was ready to receive it or not. The difficulty was in the fact that her experiences were intermittent because of the distance away in which she lived. Again, she said what she had prepared with such elegance and grace, strength and love that I could only smile knowing Mom was watching with such love.

Finally, there was me, her eldest, her caregiver, her confidant. I saw her pain, I saw her tears and cried with her. I had experienced things with Mom that I never thought I would, or even could. Again, a God who will bear us up when we cannot bear it ourselves was there for me through every turn. I spoke of Mom's love for the Lord; I spoke of her pain throughout her life as she had a life that was not easy. I spoke of her strength, and my admiration for her even during troubled times and how she handled those times with such grace. Something that she had clearly handed down to her daughters. I spoke of her love for her church and the ministries that she was called to. I spoke of her courage throughout this illness and her will to live. Finally, I told of how the Bible speaks of weeping and that it may endure for a night, but joy comes in the morning. It was time for our mom to wake up, and truly go home, for it was her morning.

As the service ended, our pastor explained the next phase of the service. The family was to be greeted by the attendees, and a viewing of my mother would be held after the service for those who wished to pay final respects in private. We had requested my mother lay in state for an hour after the service with the lights dimmed so that there would be a level of comfort in the sanctuary. Each person in attendance was handed a white balloon by the ushers and directed outside onto the church steps and in the front of the church. As we filed out, the family stood in the middle and the pastor spoke final words and Scriptures. We had requested the service end with everyone releasing the balloons as we released my mother from this earth into the arms of her Heavenly Father who was waiting for her to come home. This event literally stopped traffic, as the hundreds of people that attended this service stood outside of the church and released all of the white balloons into the sky.

As those who desired to, went back into the church for refreshments downstairs with the family, the lights had been dimmed in the sanctuary, the pictures cleared from the top of Mommy's casket and she lay softly, quietly, beautifully. Some of the people who knew our family well, and had served with Mom in different capacities at church, were initially hesitant to see her sleeping and not as the spry woman they once knew. Some of the children that had joined with my daughter and adopted her Nauni as their Nauni were afraid to see her.

Yet, a wonderful thing happened. I came upstairs from the dining room to spend a few quiet last moments with Mom and to my surprise saw my daughter at the casket with three of her closest friends at church saying, "See, she won't hurt you; she still looks like Nauni. She is just sleeping, and the rest of her is in heaven with Jesus."

As my eyes welled up with tears, I knew all things had been done well, and everyone was at peace. Finally, I could truly proclaim for Mom that with no more pain, no more suffering, only rejoicing, she was now and forever with her Heavenly Father and that there was indeed no place like home.

EPILOGUE

I f we make a concerted effort after a storm is over to look back, whether with a sigh of relief, or through a tearstained face and the sobbing sounds that nearly take our breath way, we must remember God loves us no matter what! So much so, that He sacrificed His only Son for us.

Through this experience I have been given the courage and the strength to keep my faith and to look any storm of life in the eye and know God will be there. Through this experience, I was given the opportunity to witness the power of forgiveness through my mother on her last Christmas, and to experience forgiveness through the years of a turbulent mother-daughter relationship that completely changed as my mother's caregiver. God gave me the capacity to show forgiveness to a man whose only way of dealing with his wife's illness, was not to deal with it at all and the compassion to see the humanity in him.

Finally, God gave me the understanding and the acceptance of how He chose to heal in this situation. Healing does not always come in the form that we want or expect. God still chose to heal my mother, but He chose to call her home for her glorious and ultimate healing.